THE ULTIMATE

HOW TO DRAW
CUTE STUFF IN
5 MIINUTES

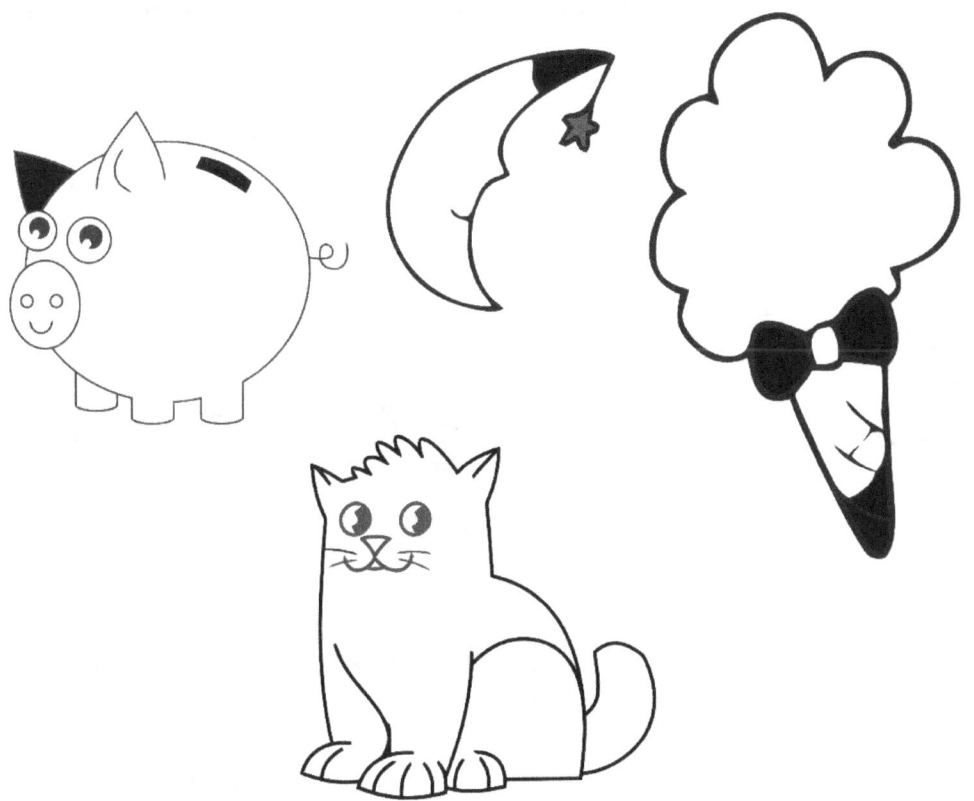

Nevaeh caddel

THIS BOOK BELONGS TO

NAME

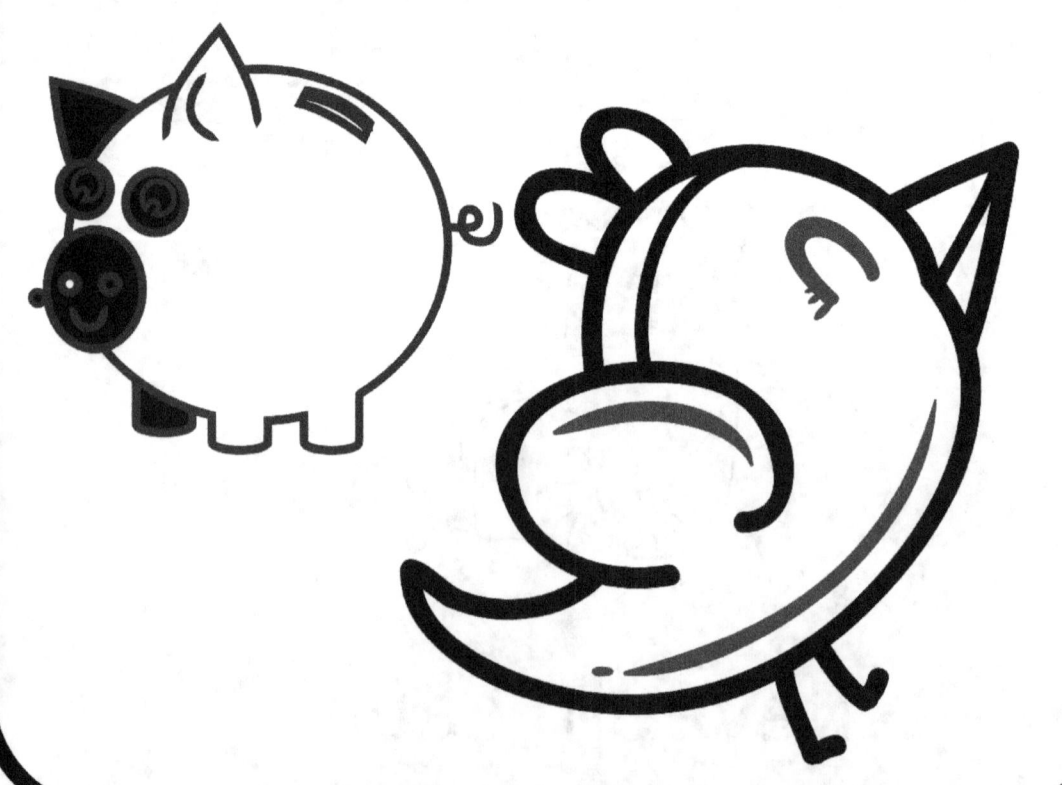

INTROUCTION

Nicholas, a talented artist with a passion for spreading creativity among children, embarked on a mission to create "The Ultimate How to Draw Cute Stuff in 5 Minutes for Kids" book. His journey began when he noticed the joy and wonder that simple drawings brought to his niece and nephew. Determined to ignite this same spark in young hearts everywhere, he dedicated himself to the project.

Nicholas delved into weeks of research, exploring the interests of children and their favorite characters. He carefully honed his drawing skills, ensuring his creations were both adorable and accessible to kids of all ages. Late nights were spent perfecting every stroke and character, from cuddly animals to whimsical monsters.

As he completed each illustration, Nicholas shared them with his little testers, incorporating their feedback to make the drawings even more engaging. He infused the book with step-by-step instructions, breaking down complex characters into manageable steps. His dedication paid off when he saw the radiant smiles of children learning to draw with ease.

The Ultimate How to Draw Cute Stuff in 5 Minutes for Kids became a hit, inspiring countless young artists and fostering their creativity. Nicholas had not only fulfilled his dream but had also kindled the artistic flames in a generation of children, leaving a heartwarming legacy for years to come.

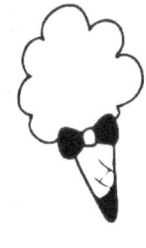

THE ULTIMATE
HOW TO DRAW
CUTE STUFF IN
5 MIINUTES

Step 1: Gather Supplies
Begin by collecting essential drawing materials, such as blank sheets of paper, pencils, erasers, and a set of colored Pencils or crayons. Ensure the workspace is well-lit and comfortable.

Step 2: Basic Shapes
Teach kids to start with basic shapes like circles, squares, triangles, and rectangles. These can serve as building blocks for more complex drawings.

Step 3: Lines and Doodles
Introduce the concept of different lines straight, curved, zigzag, and dashed. Encourage kids to practice making various lines and doodles to improve their hand-eye coordination.

Step 4: Simple Objects
Guide them in drawing simple objects like apples, stars, and hearts using the basic shapes and lines they've learned. Keep these early drawings straightforward to build confidence.

Step 5: Animals and Characters
Move on to drawing easy animals or characters like cats, dogs, and smiley faces. Use basic shapes and lines as a foundation, and add details like eyes, mouths, and tails.

Step 6: Nature and Scenery
Introduce kids to drawing nature scenes like trees, flowers, and the sun. These can be created using simple shapes and lines, and colored in with crayons.

Step 7: Coloring
Explain the concept of coloring within the lines, using various shades to make drawings more vibrant. Encourage creativity in choosing colors.

Step 8: Practice
Emphasize the importance of practice. Kids should continue drawing regularly to improve their skills. Provide blank pages for them to express their ideas freely.

The wonderful thing about art is that you may use whatever tool you desire! Yes, that's correct! Because you are the artist, feel free to get creative with this book, but keep it simple. It's simple to learn if you use blank sheets of paper or grind paper.

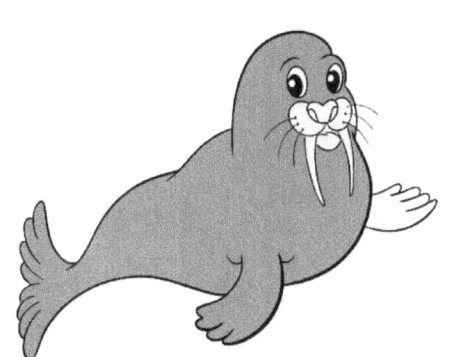

When learning to draw, all you actually need is a pencil and a good eraser. To follow the step-by-step directions, first sketch everything gently, then go over your lines with any tool you like. on add details on your animal, you can use various pens, markers, colored pencils, or even crayons.

DOTS

Make some dots in the space below.

● ● ● ● ● ● ●

● ● ● ● ● ● ●

● ● ● ● ● ● ●

_____

Study and scribble towards clockwise direction here.

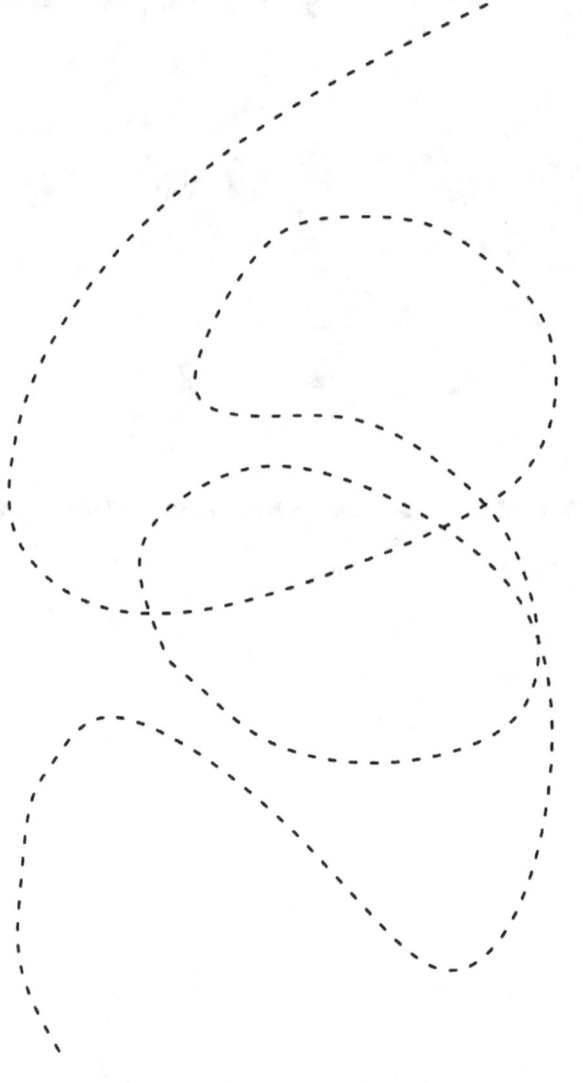

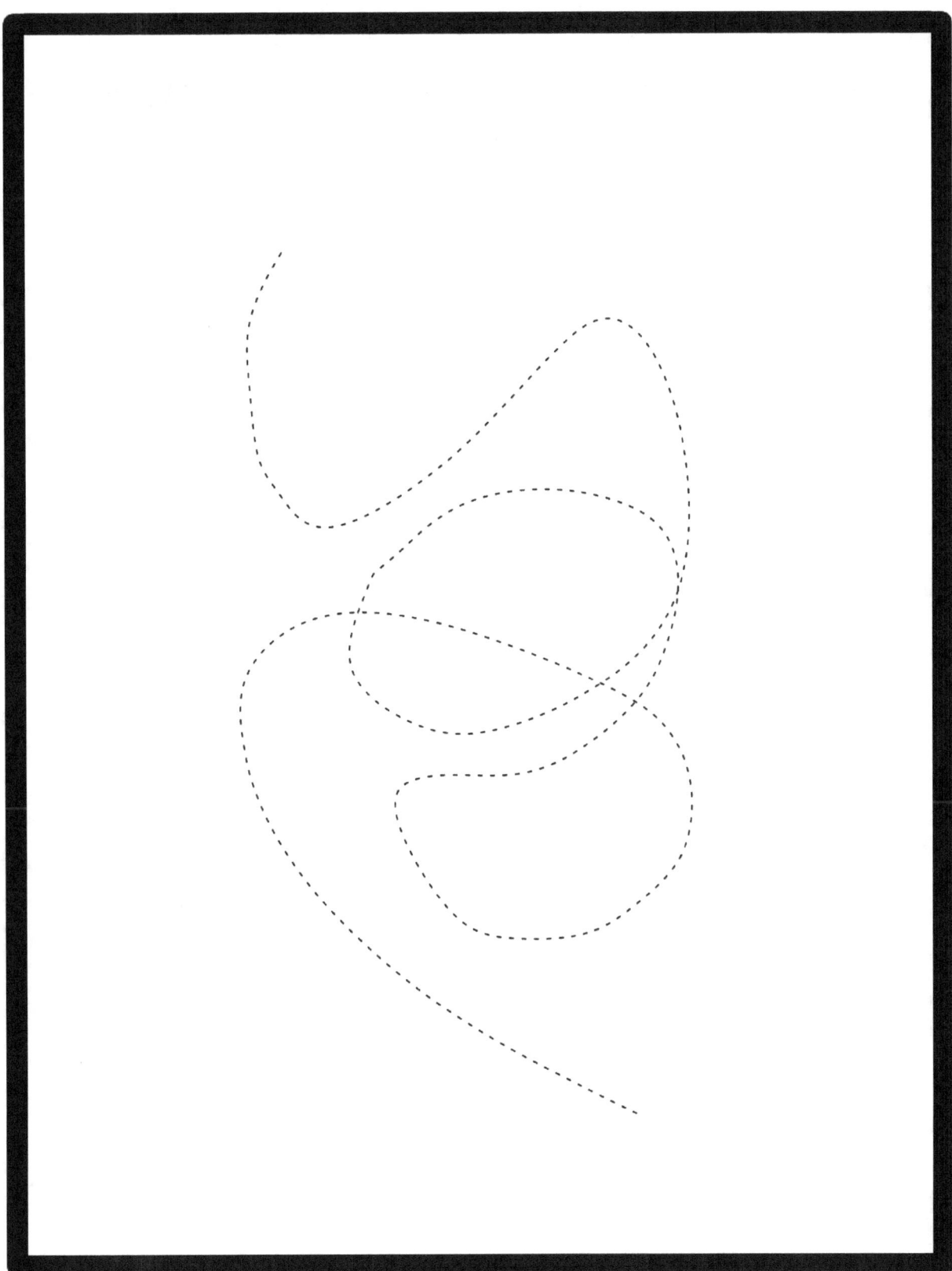

Trace and make the clockwise patterns below.

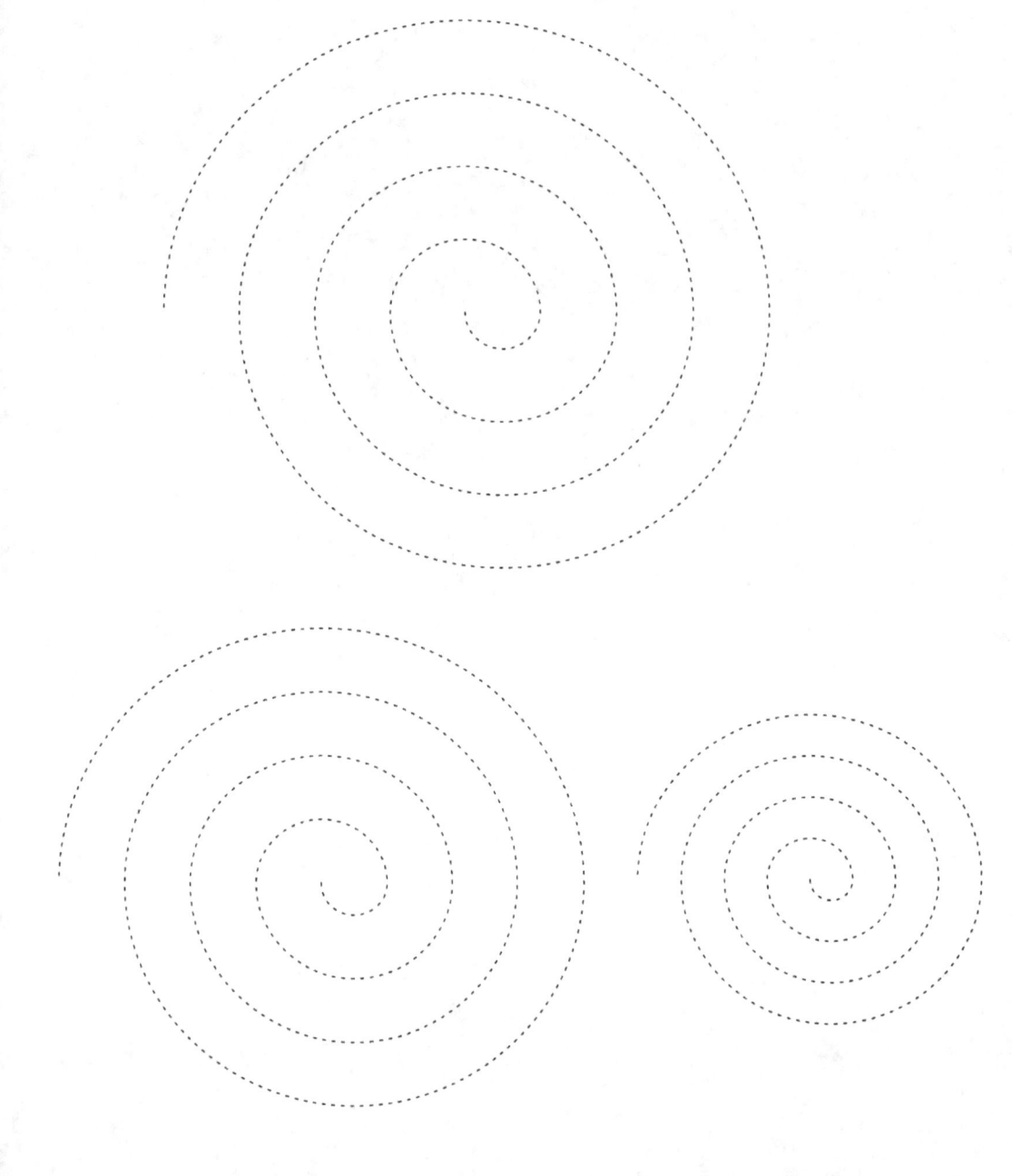

Trace and make the clockwise patterns below.

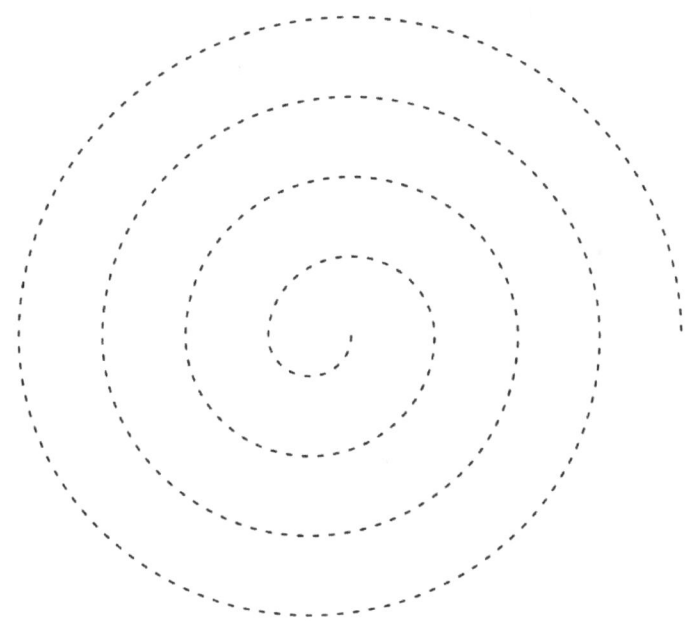

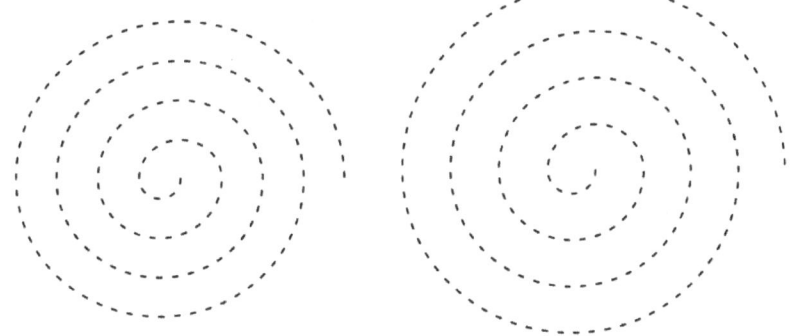

HORIZONTAL LINES

Trace the horizontal lines.

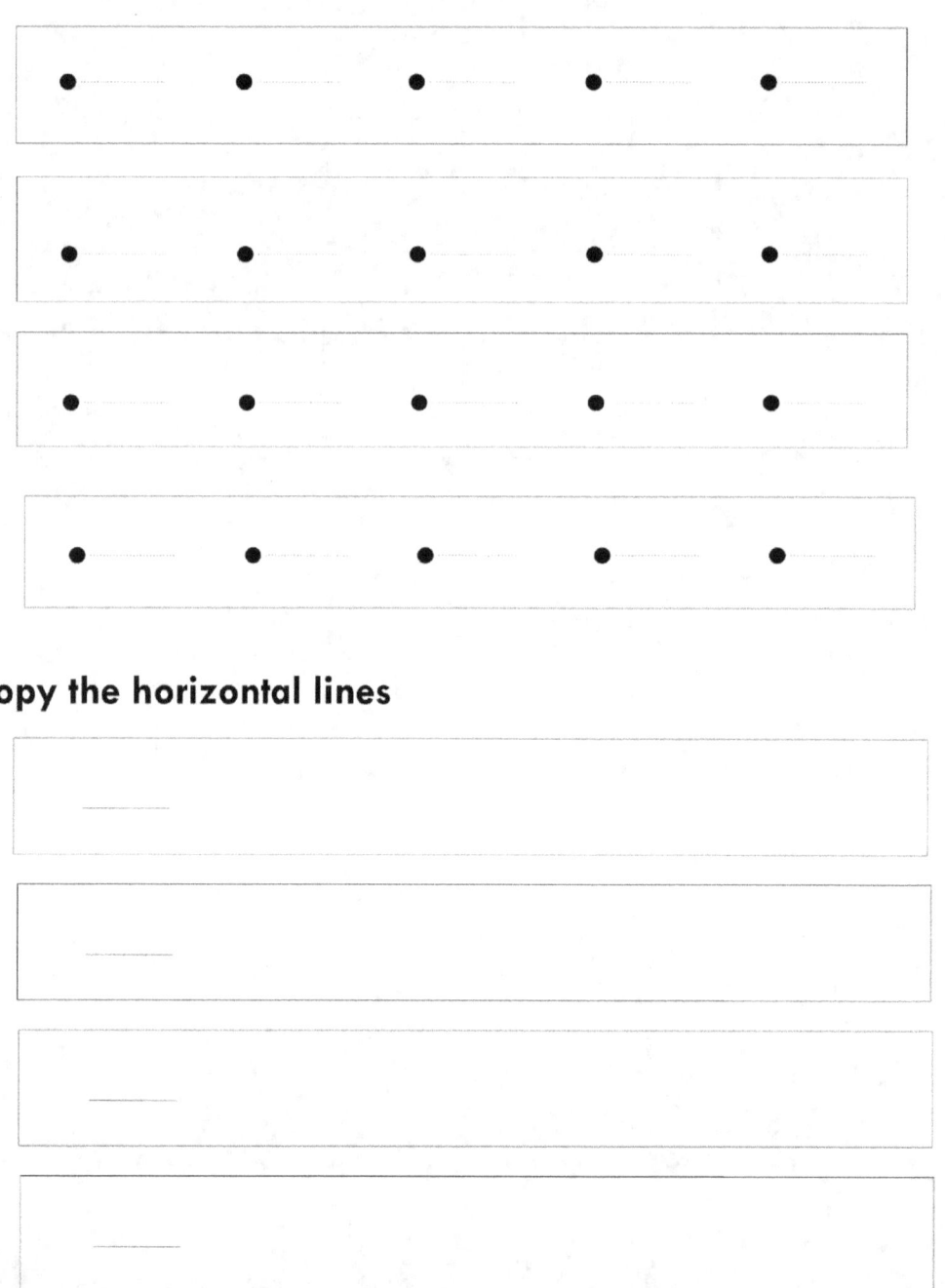

Copy the horizontal lines

Trace the zigzag lines.

copy the zigzag lines.

ZIGZAG LINES

Trace the zigzag lines.

copy the zigzag lines.

ZIGZAG LINES

Trace the zigzag lines.

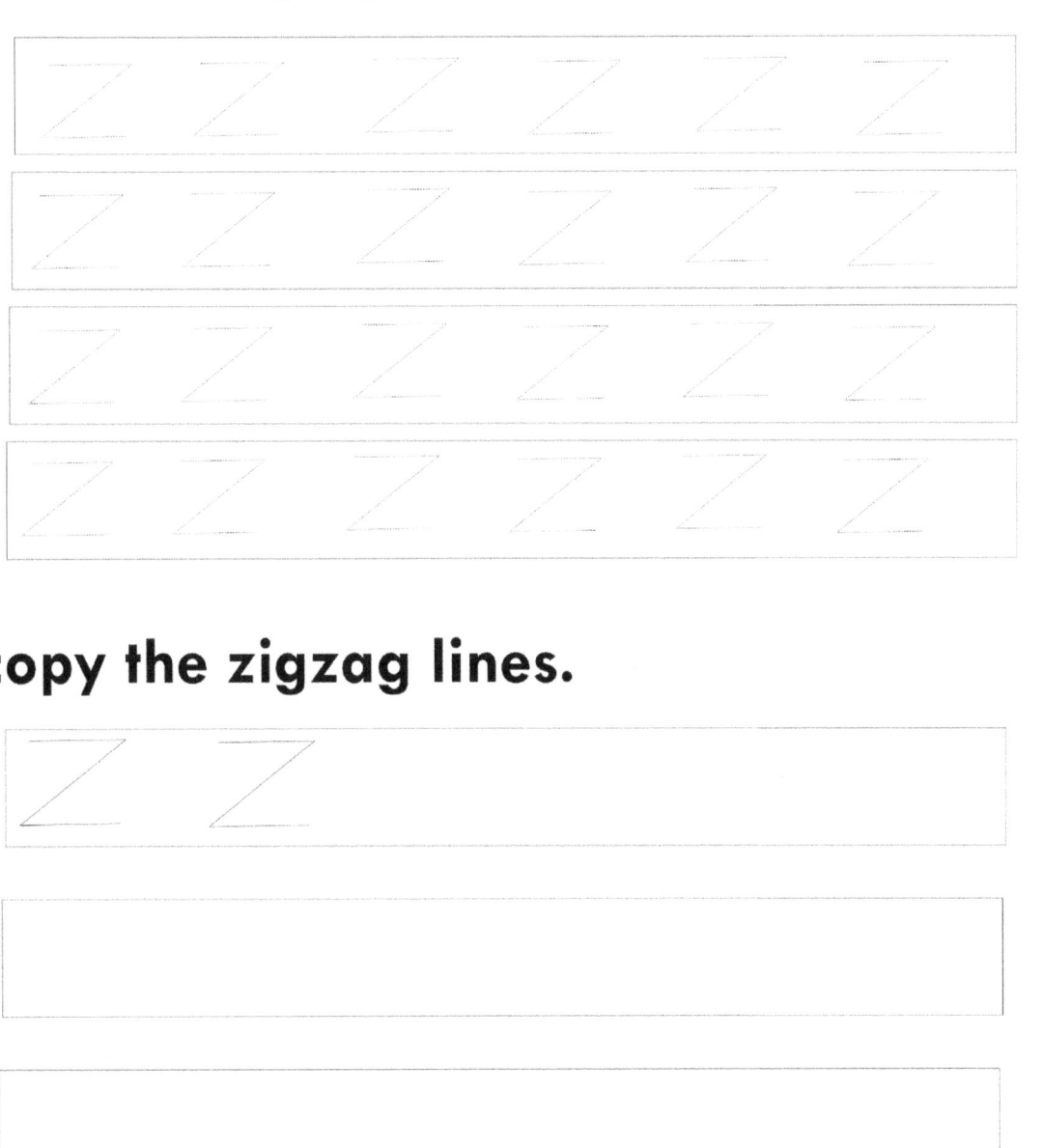

copy the zigzag lines.

HAND MOVEMENT

Trace each circle and draw your own in the space provided

Make your own circle here.

Trace the right curves.

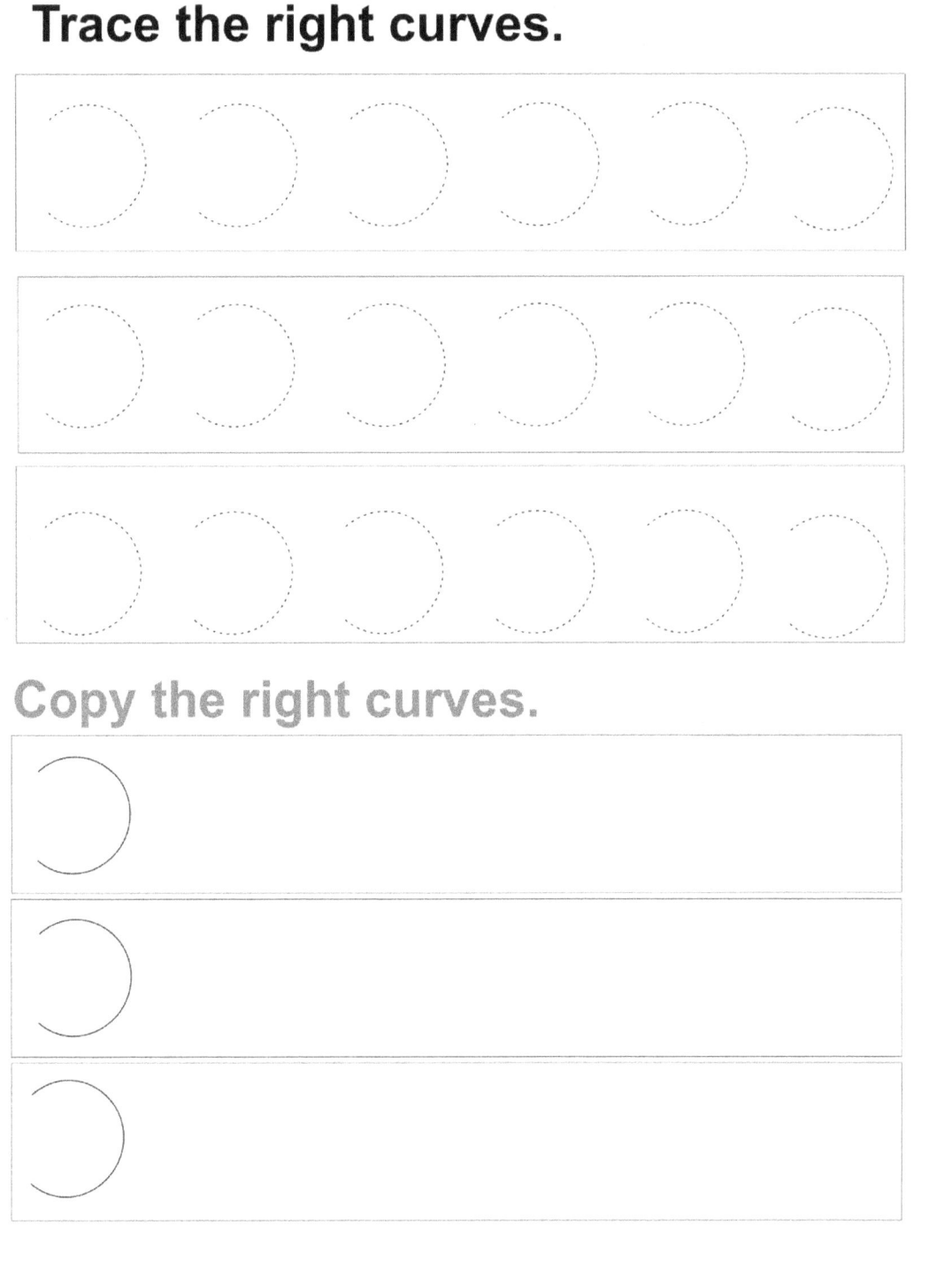

Copy the right curves.

Trace The Left Curves.

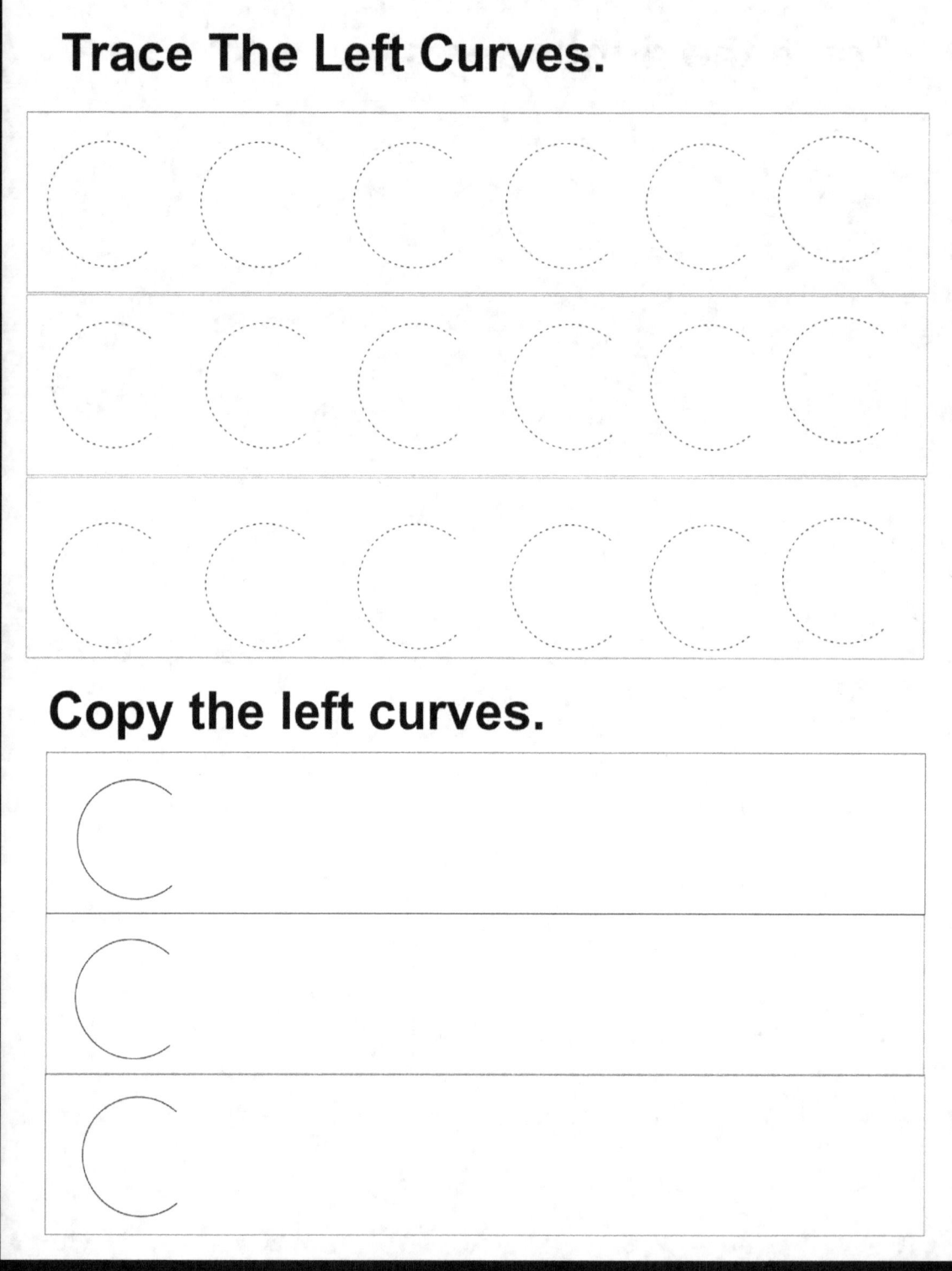

Copy the left curves.

Trace and make the pattern below.

Copy the pattern below.

Trace overlapping circles

Copy the overlaping curves.

Aa   Apple

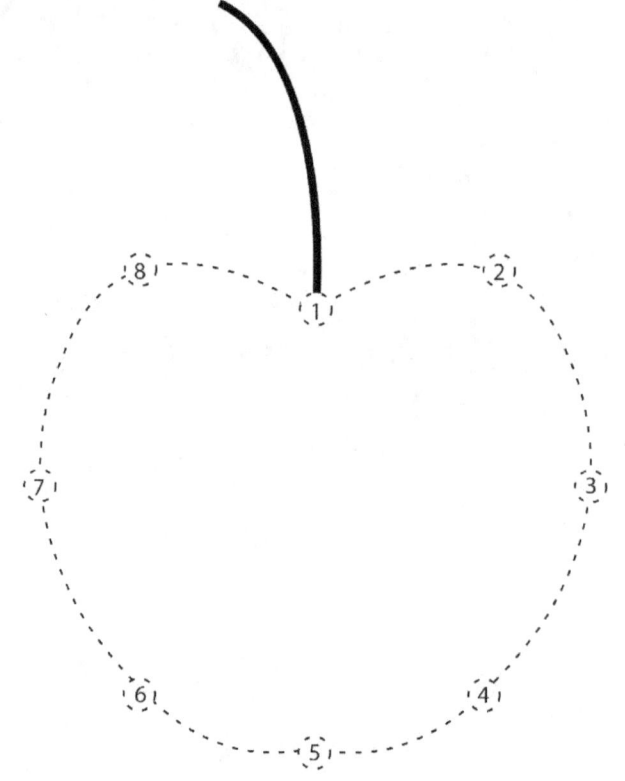

Apple = 1+2+3+4+5+6+7+8+1

Apply Red color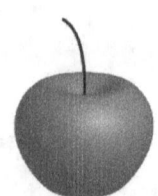

Self Practice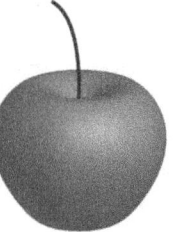

Bb

Ball

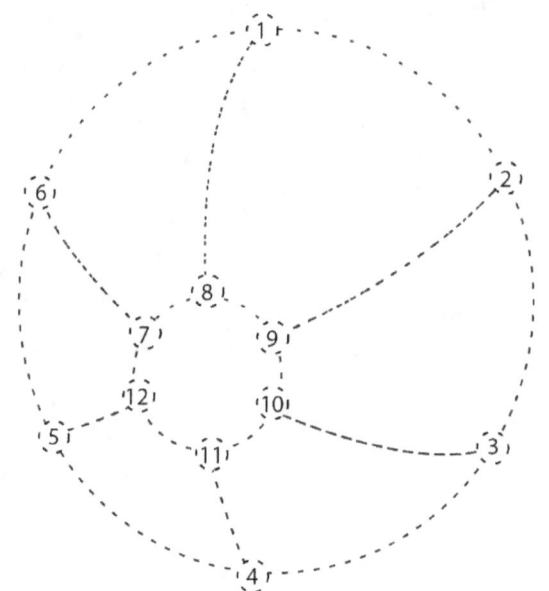

Ball = 1+2+3+4+5+6+1
and 6+7+8+9+10+11+12
and 8+1, 9+2, 10+3, 11+4, 12+5

Apply Green, Orange, and Blue color

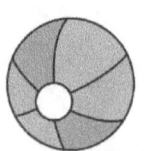

Self Practice

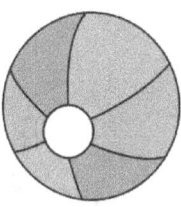

Cc

Cap

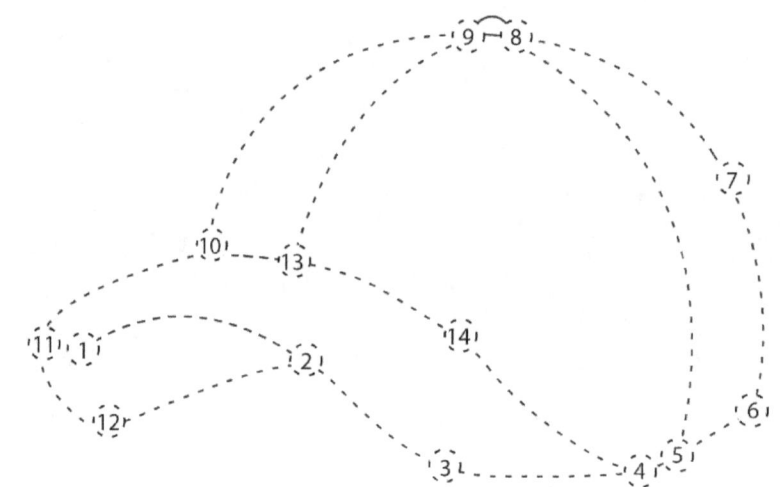

Cap = 1+2+3+4+5+6+7+8+9+10+11+12+1
and 10+13+14+4 and 13+9
and 8+5

Apply Red and Blue color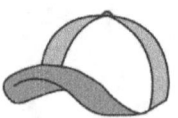

Self Practice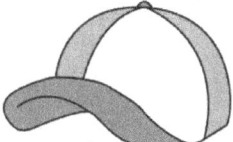

Dd Duck

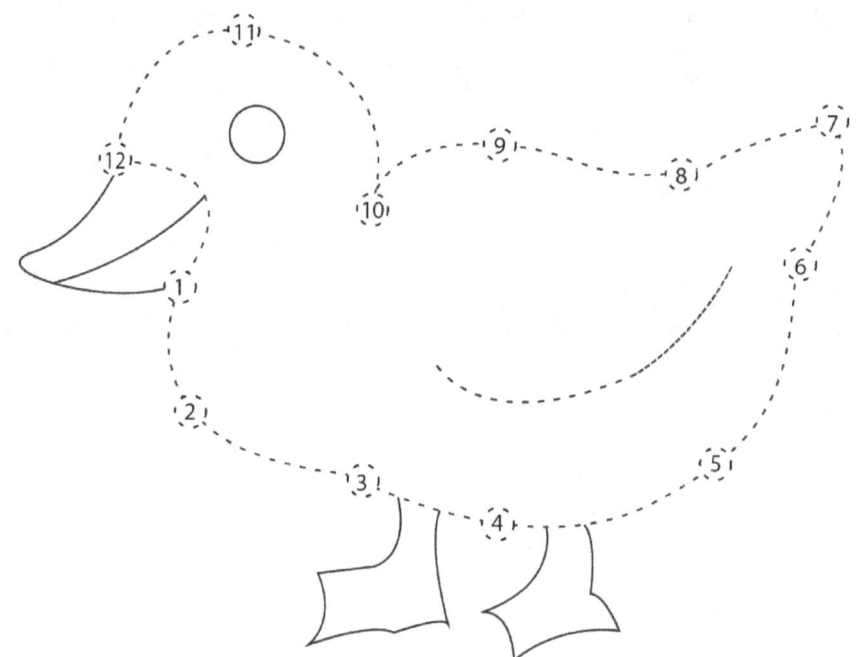

Duck = 1+2+3+4+5+6+7+8+9+10+11+12+1

Apply Yellow and Orange color

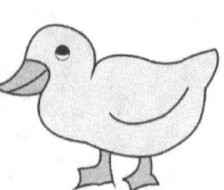

Self Practice

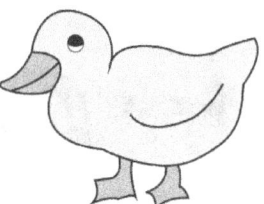

Ee Elephant

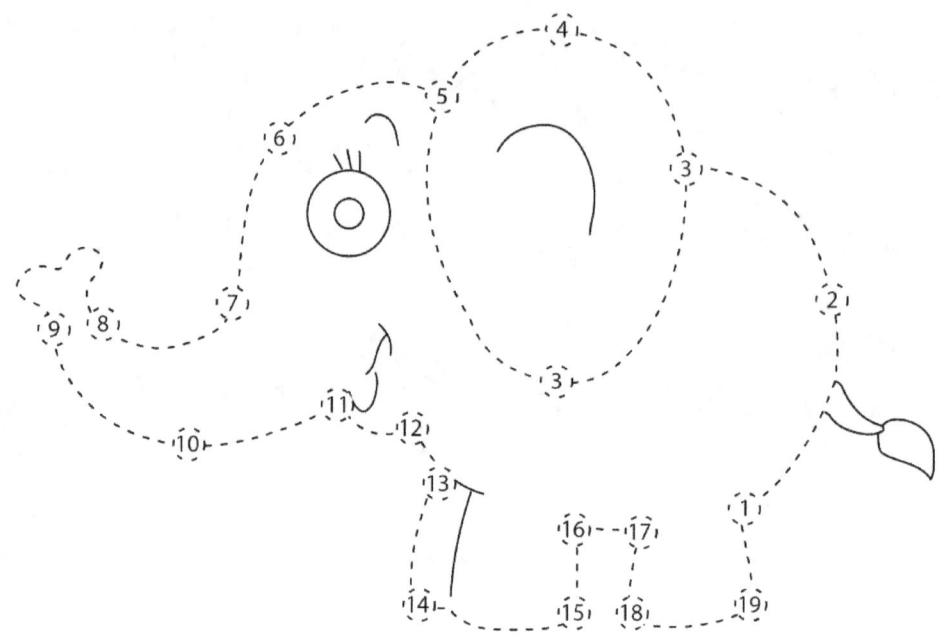

Elephant = 1+2+3+4+5+6+7+8+9+10+11+12+
13+14+15+16+17+18+19+1

Apply Light Black color

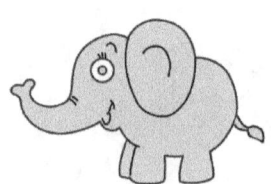

Self Practice

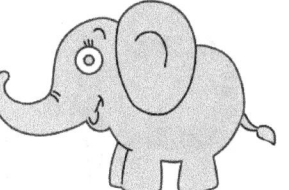

Ff

Fish

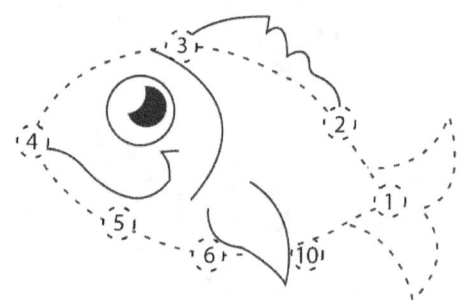

Fish = 1+2+3+4+5+6+1
and 6+7+8+9+10+11+12
and 8+1, 9+2, 10+3, 11+4, 12+5

Apply Orange Color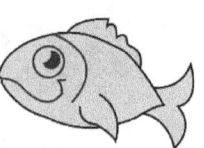

Self Practice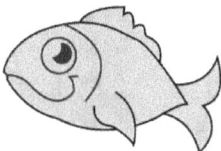

Gg Giraffe

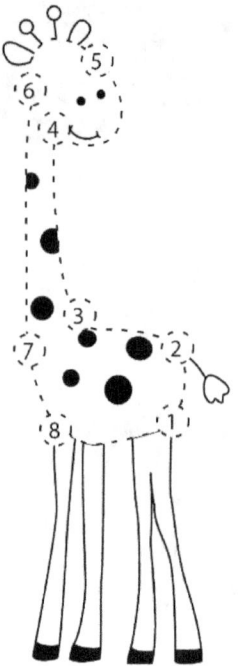

Giraffe = 1+2+3+4+5+6+1
and 6+7+8+9+10+11+12
and 8+1, 9+2, 10+3, 11+4, 12+5

Apply Orange Color

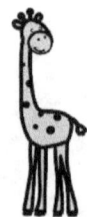

Self Practice

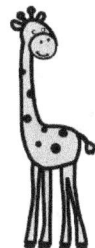

Hh Horse

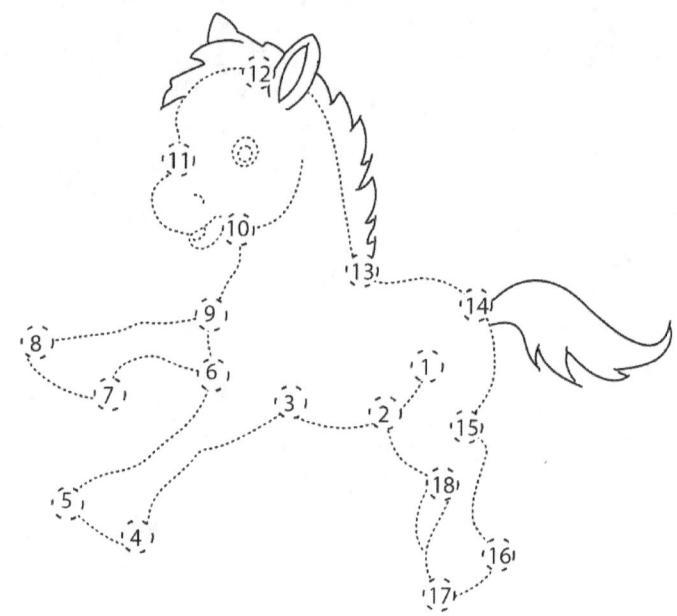

Horse = 1+2+3+4+5+6+7+8+9+10+11+12+13+
14+15+16+17+18+2
and 6+9

Apply Broun and White Broun Color

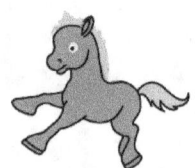

Self Practice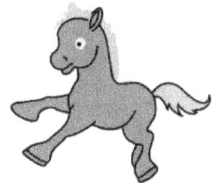

Ii

Ice Cream

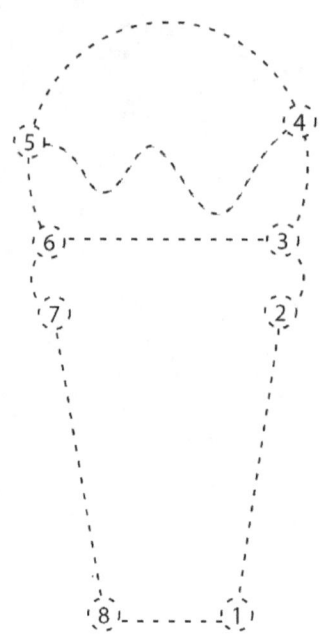

Ice Cream = 1+2+3+4+5+6+7+8+1
and 3+6, and 2+7

Apply Red, Chocolate and orange color

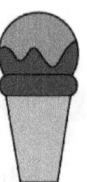

Self Practice

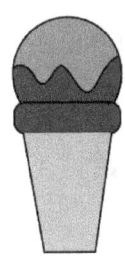

Jj

Jar

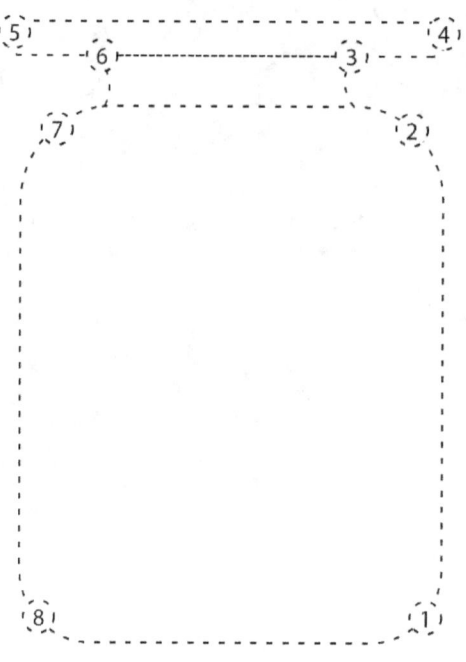

Jar = 1+2+3+4+5+6+7+8+1
and 3+6

Apply Blue, Pink color

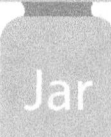

Self Practice

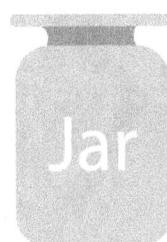

Kk

Kite

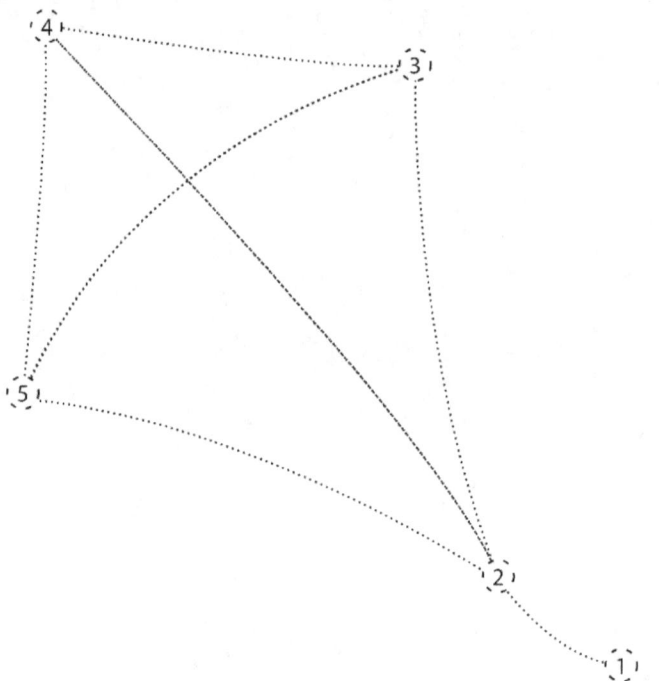

Kite = 1+2+3+4+5+2
and 2+4 and 3+5

Apply Red, Green, yellow and Blue color

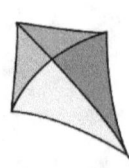

Self Practice

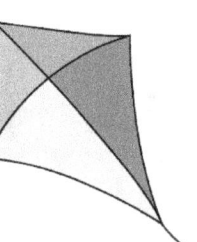

Ll

Leaf

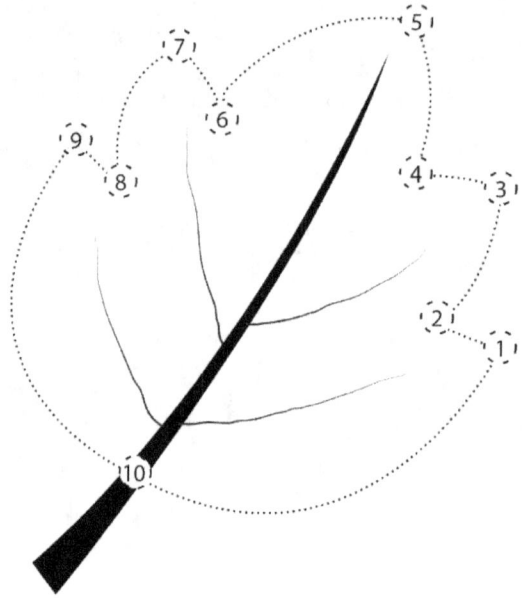

Leaf = 1+2+3+4+5+6+7+8+9+10+1

Apply Green color

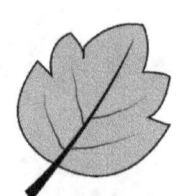

Self Practice

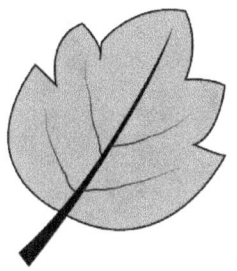

Mm Mango

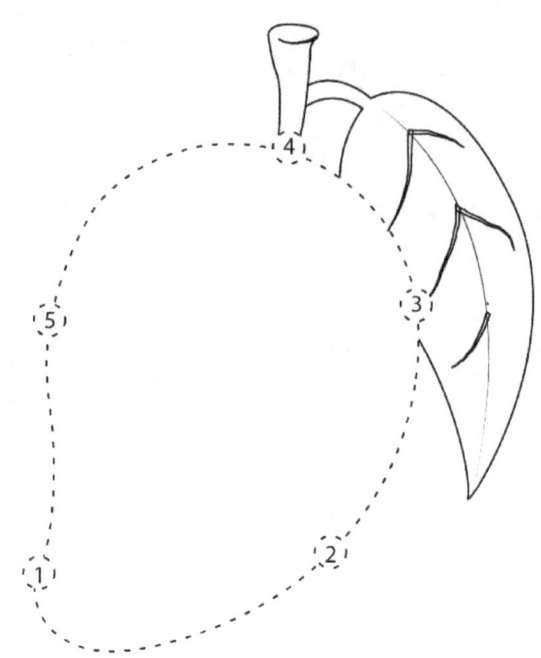

Mango = 1+2+3+4+5+1

Apply Yellow, Orange and Green color

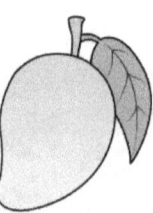

Self Practice

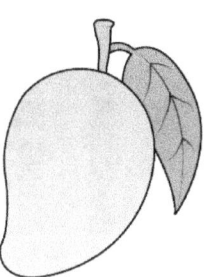

Nn   Net

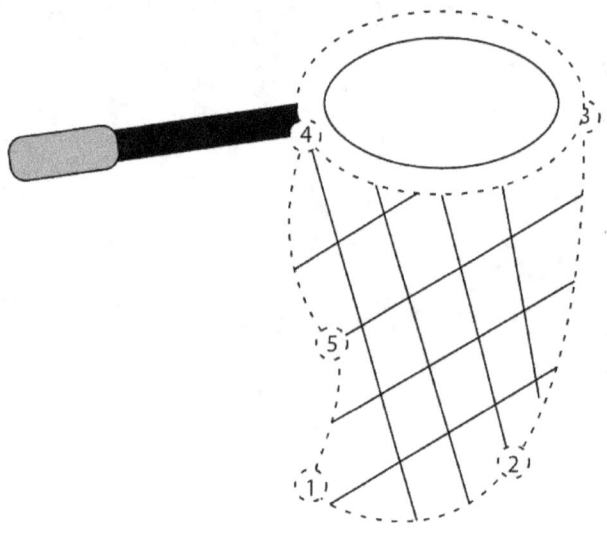

Net = 1+2+3+4+5+1

Apply White Blue color

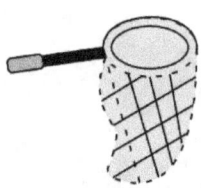

Self Practice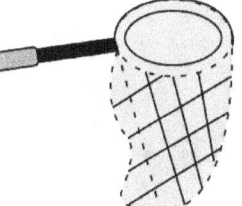

Oo   Olive

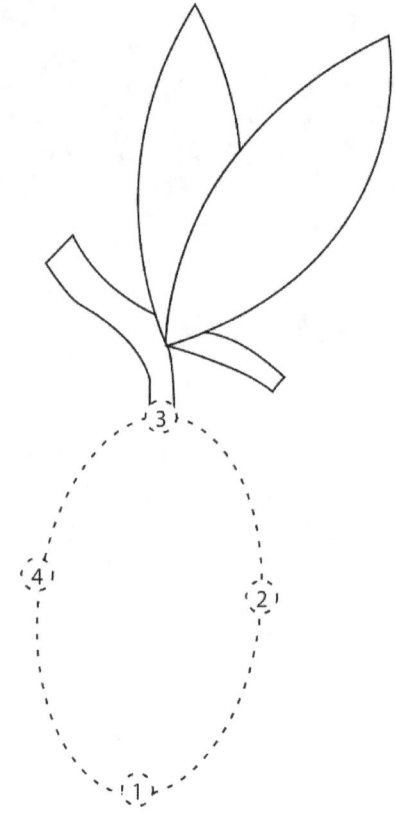

Olive = 1+2+3+4+1

Apply Green and Brown Color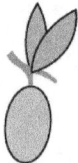

Self Practice

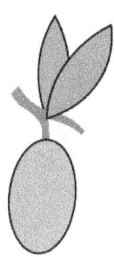

Pp   Parrot

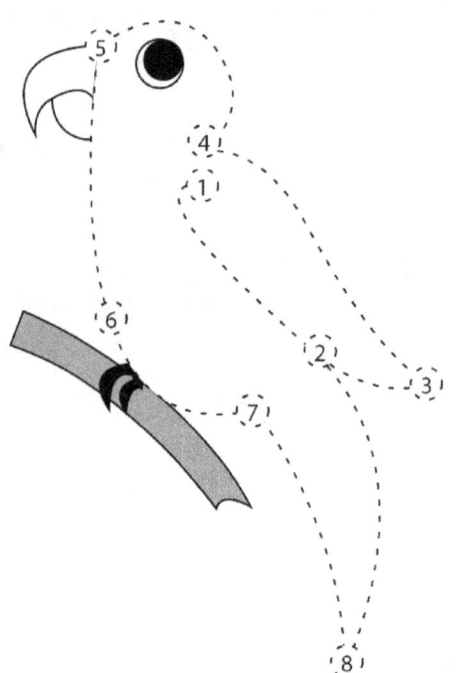

Parrot = 1+2+3+4+5+6+7+8+2

Apply Green and Red Color

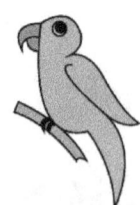

Self Practice

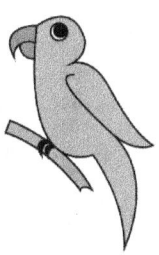

Qq Quail

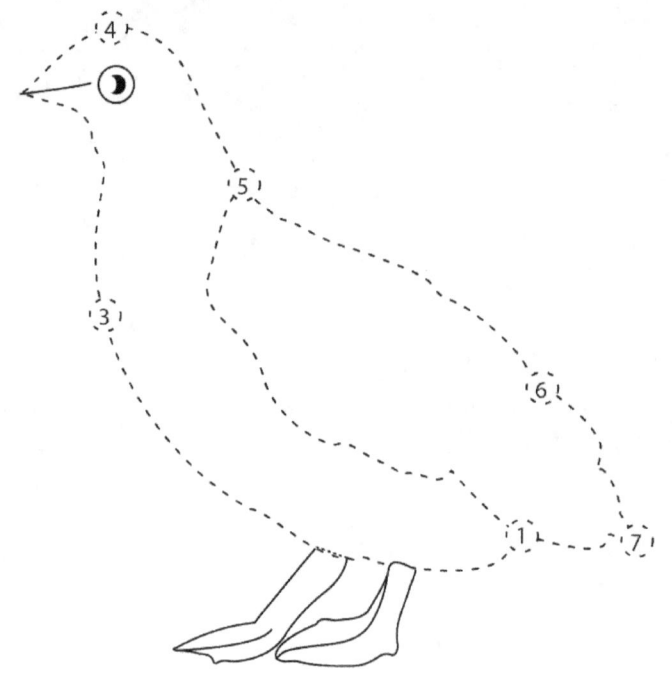

Quail = 1+2+3+4+5+6+7+1
and 1+5

Apply Brown color

Self Practice

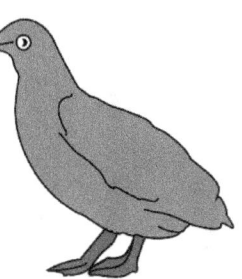

Rr   Rabbit

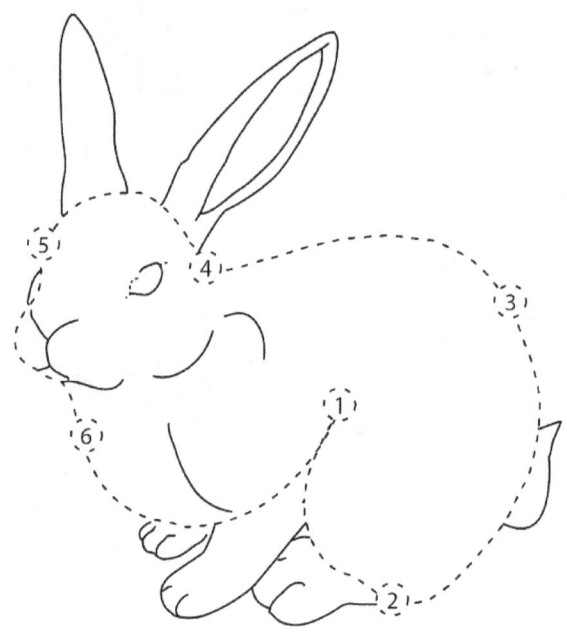

Rabbit = 1+2+3+4+5++6+1

Apply Blackwhite color

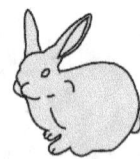

Self Practice

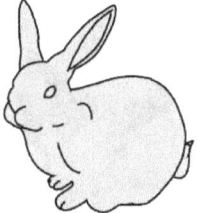

S s   Sun

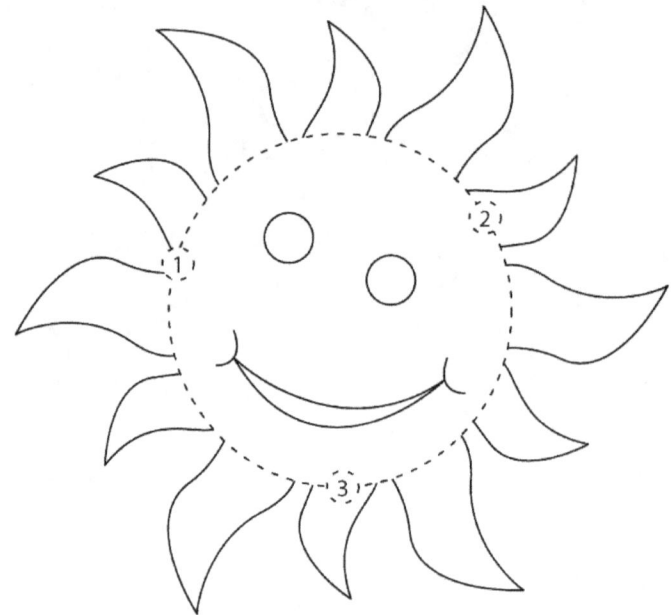

Sun = 1+2+3

Apply Orange and Yellow color

Self Practice

Tt   Tree

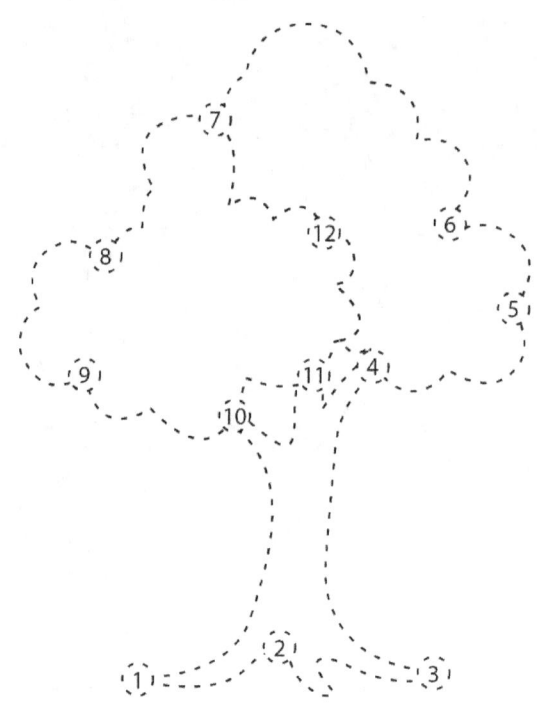

Tree = 1+2+3+4+5+6+7+8+9+10+1
and 10+11+12+7

Apply Green and Brown color

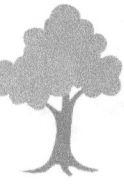

Self Practice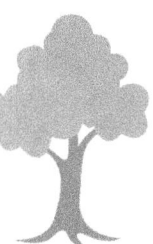

U u Umbrella

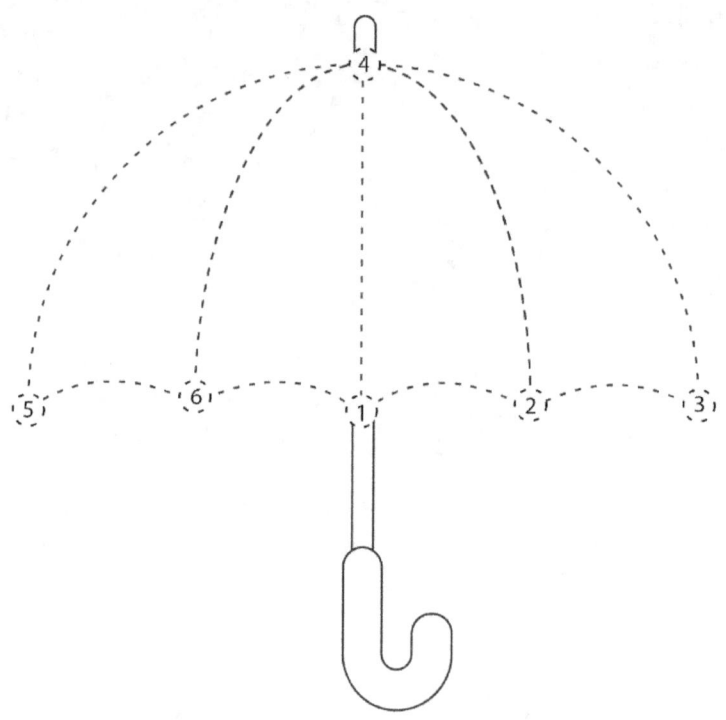

Umbrella = 1+2+3+4+5+6+1
and 2+4, 4+6

Apply Green, Orange, Pink and Blue Color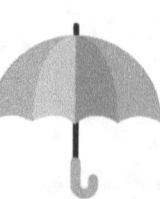

Self Practice

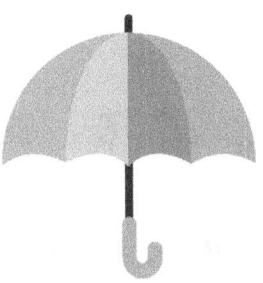

Vv　Vase

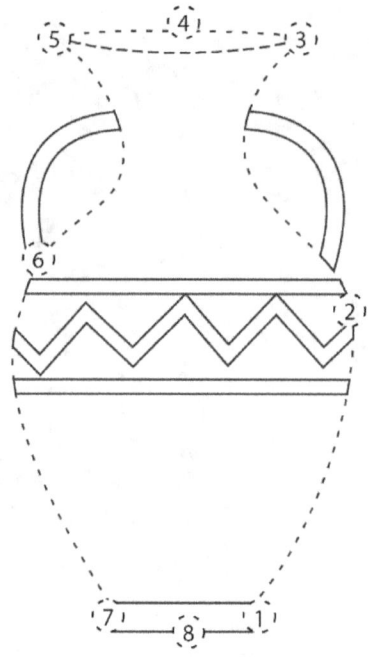

Vase = 1+2+3+4+5+6+7+8+1
and 1+7, 3+5

Apply Orange, Red, Durk Orange Color

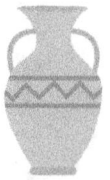

Self Practice

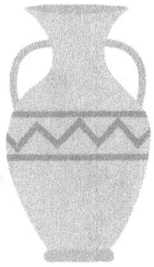

Ww Window

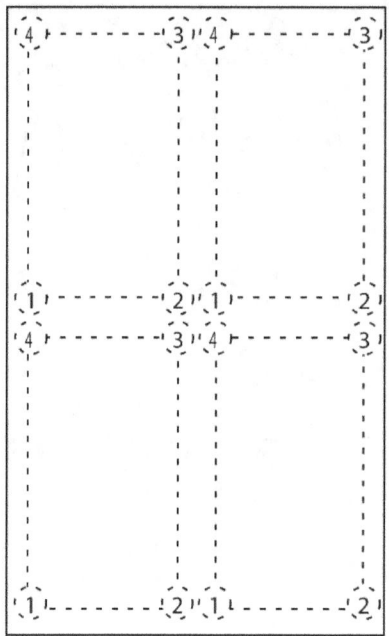

Window = 1+2+3+4 and 1+2+3+4
and 1+2+3+4 and 1+2+3+4

Apply Blue Color

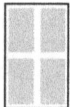

Self Practice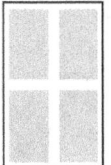

Xx Ximenia

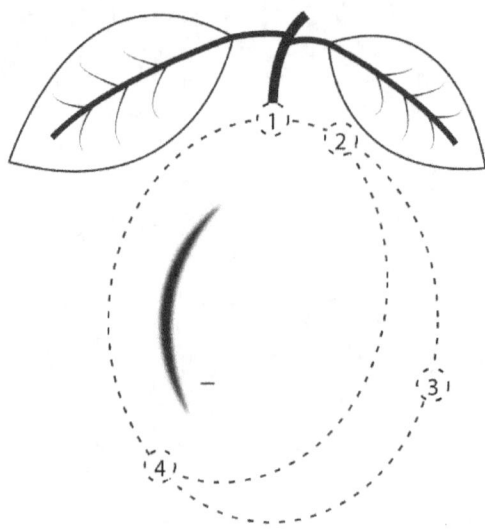

Ximenia = 1+2+3+4+1
and 2+4

Apply OrangeColor

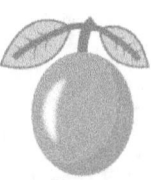

Self Practice

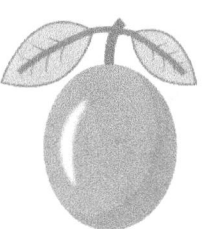

Yy

Yo-Yo

4

2

3

3

1

1

2

Yo-Yo = 1+2+3
and a+2+3+4 and 2+4

Apply Green and White Green Color

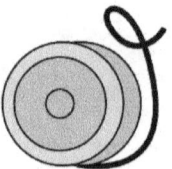

Self Practice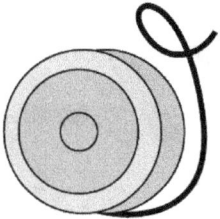

Zz

Zebra

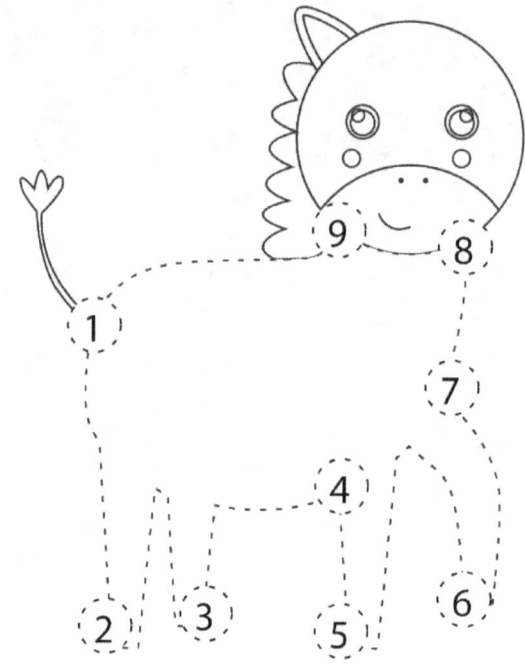

Zebra = 1+2+3+4+5+6+7+8+9+1

Apply Black and Red Color

Self Practice

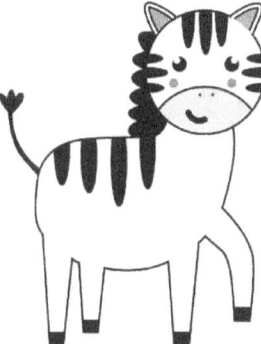

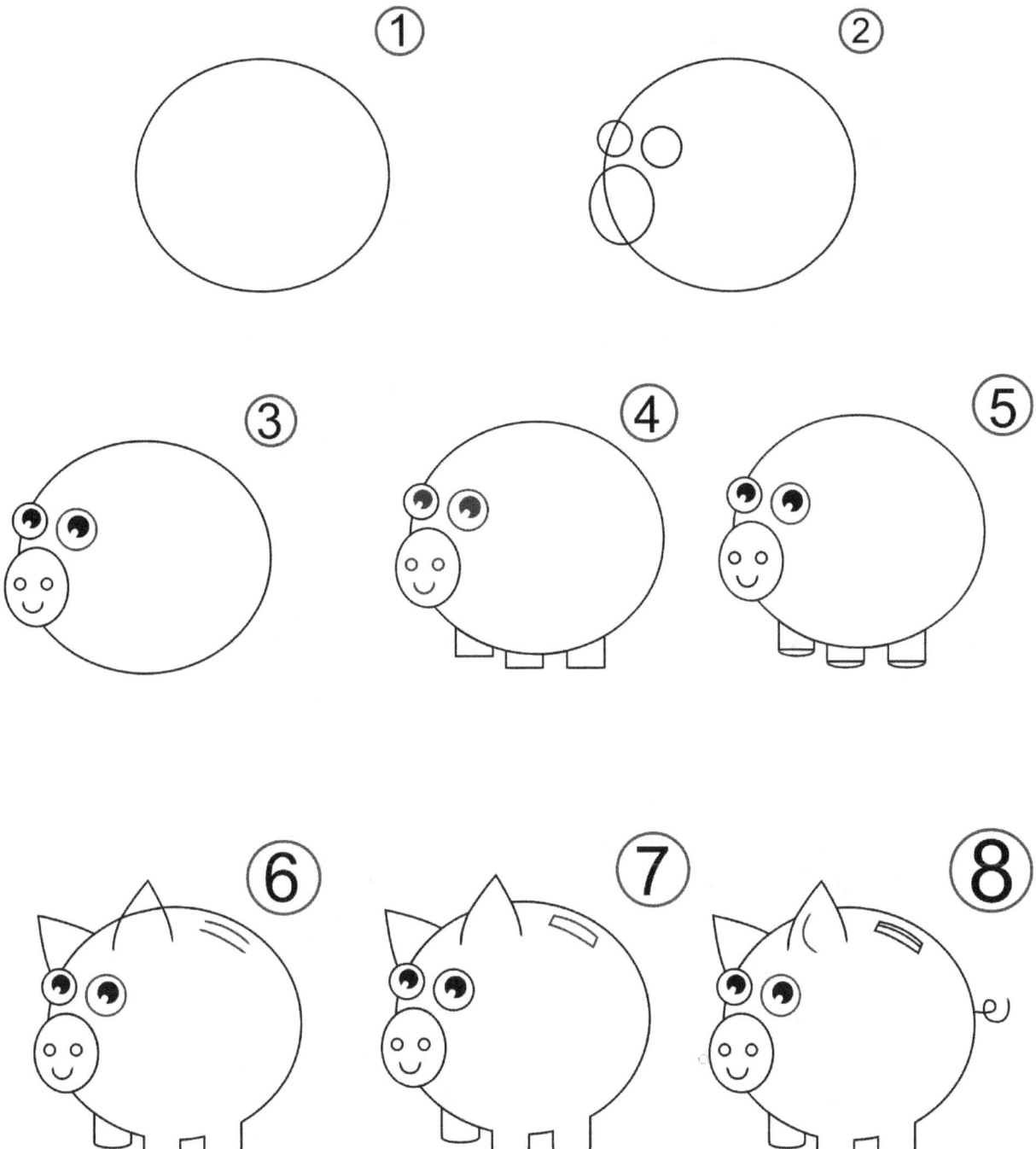

BIRD

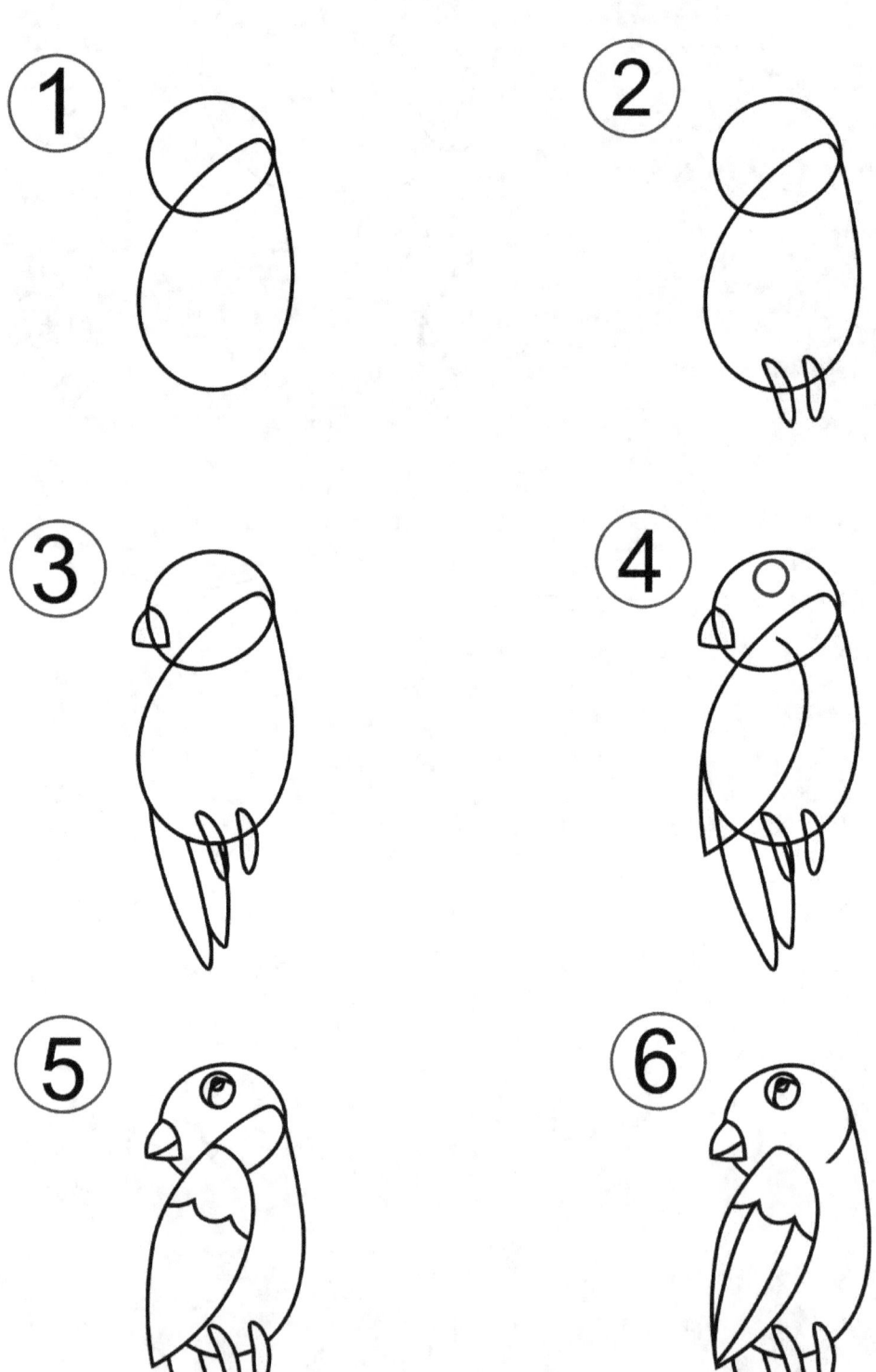

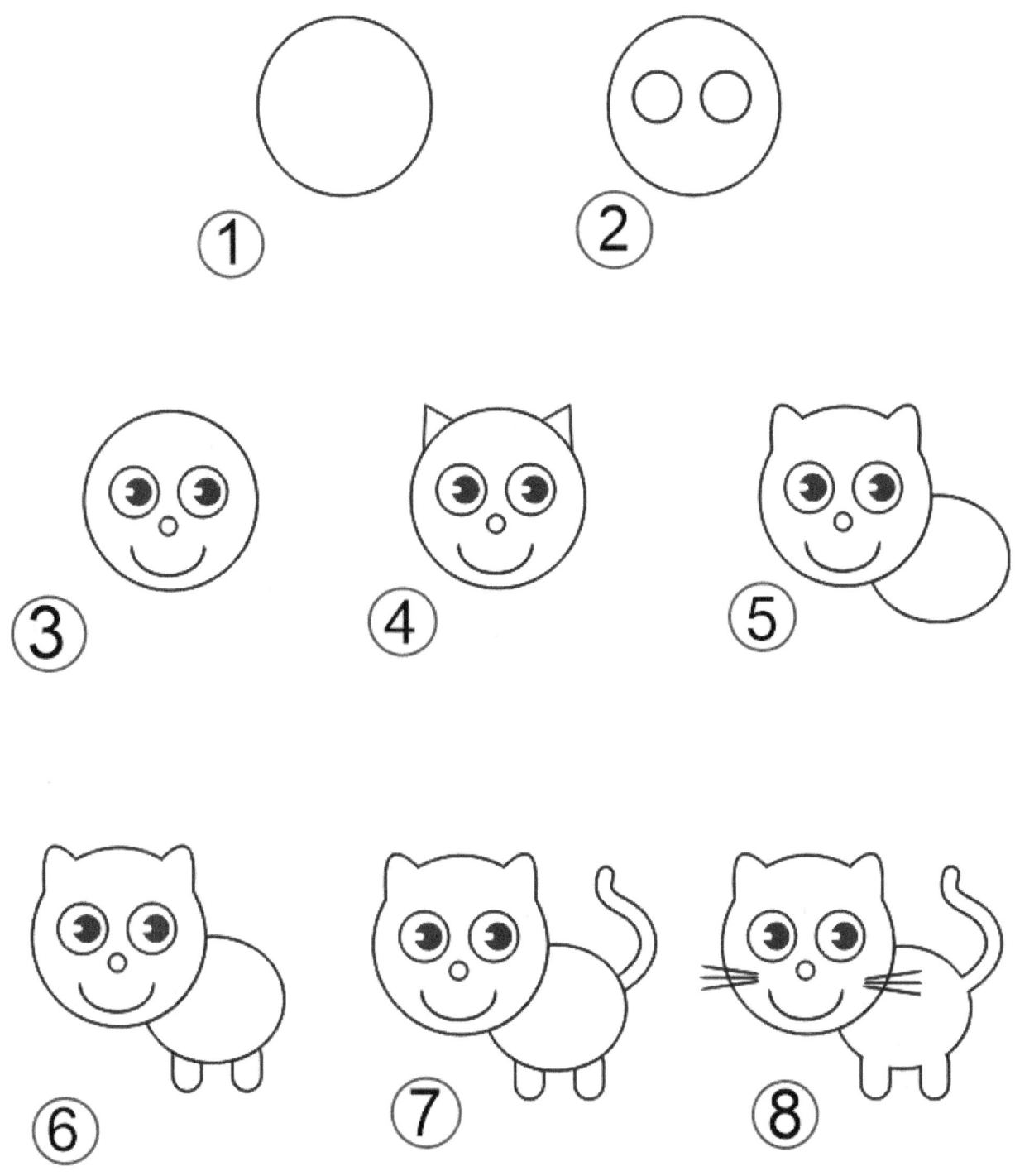

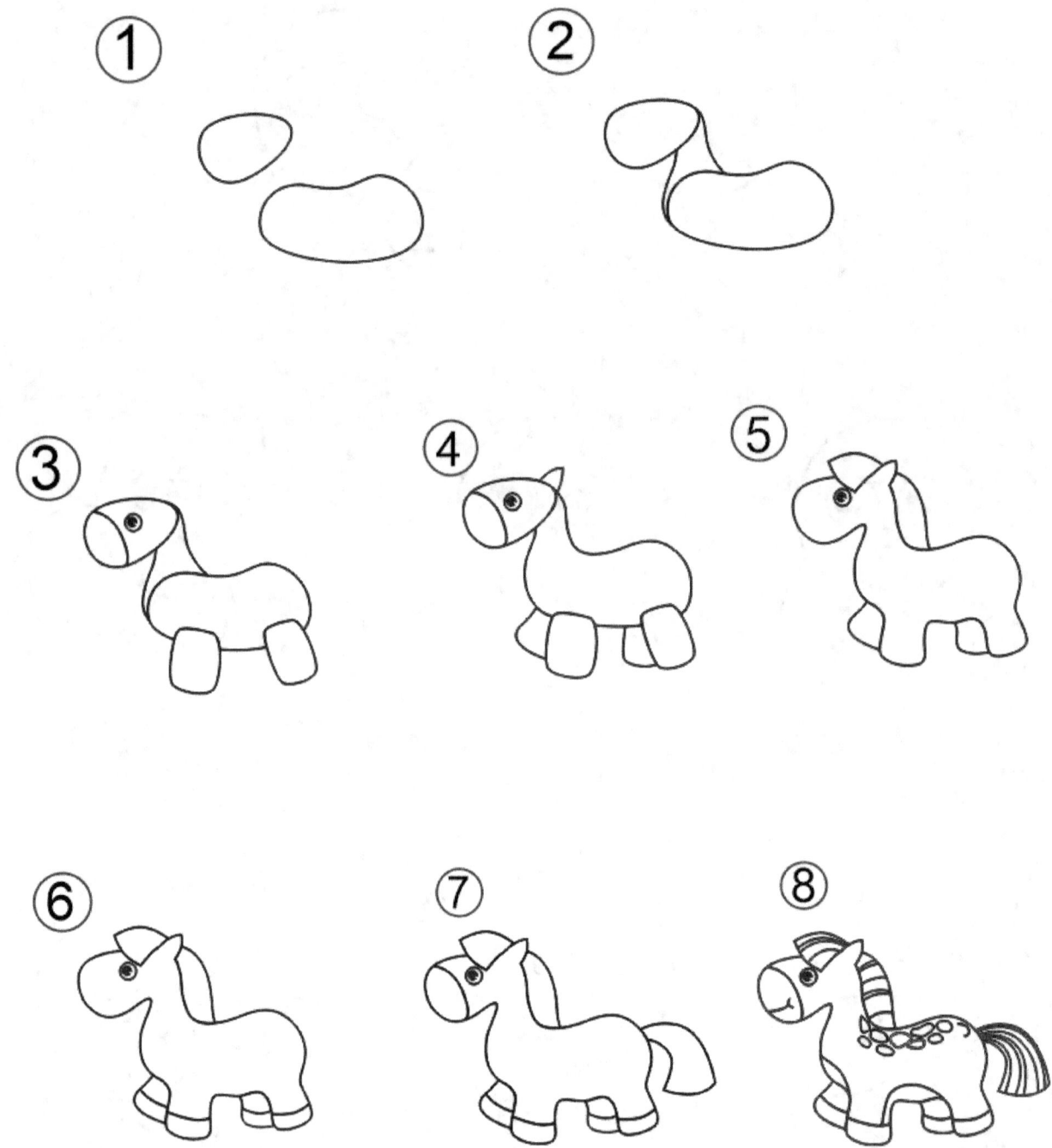

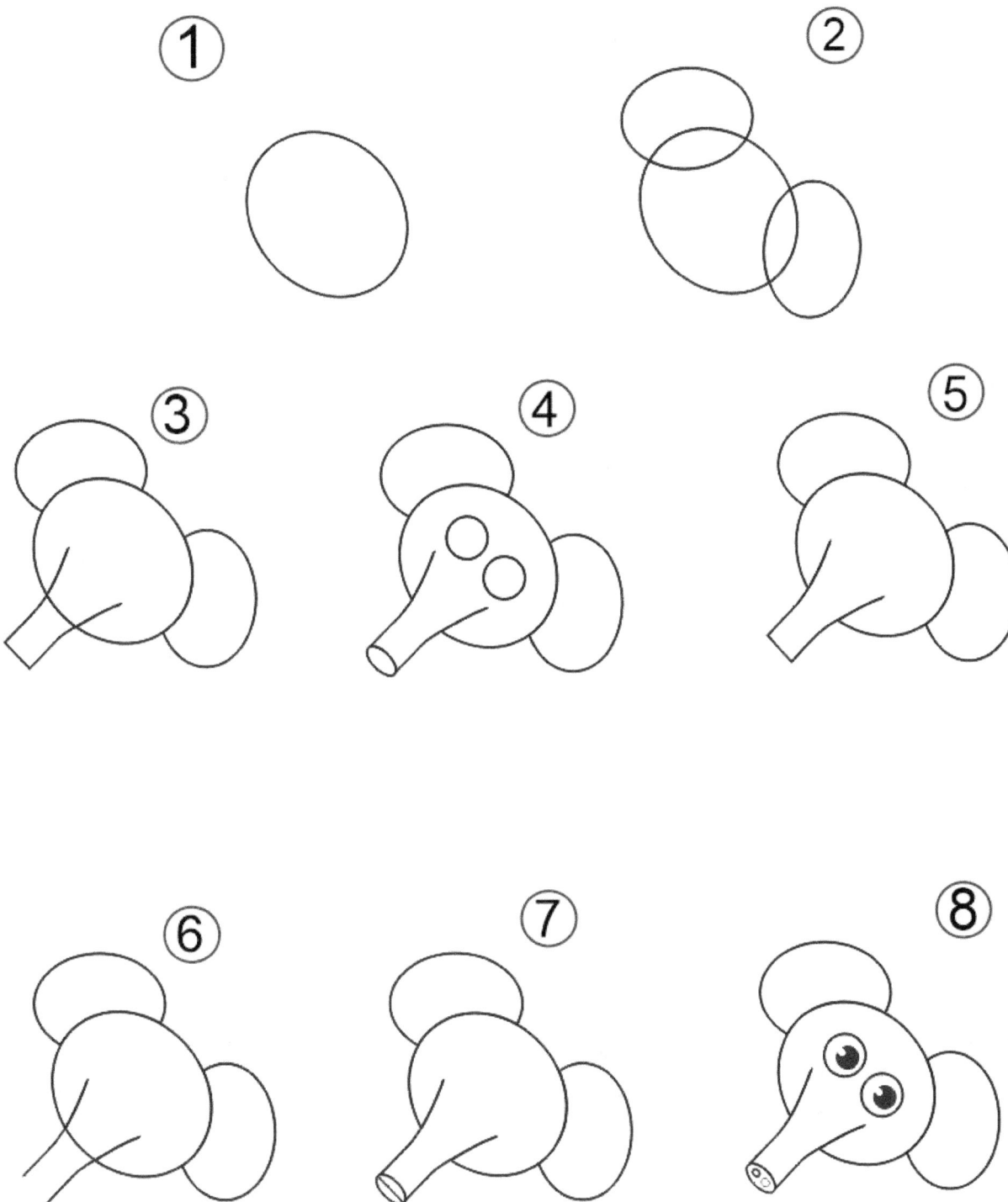

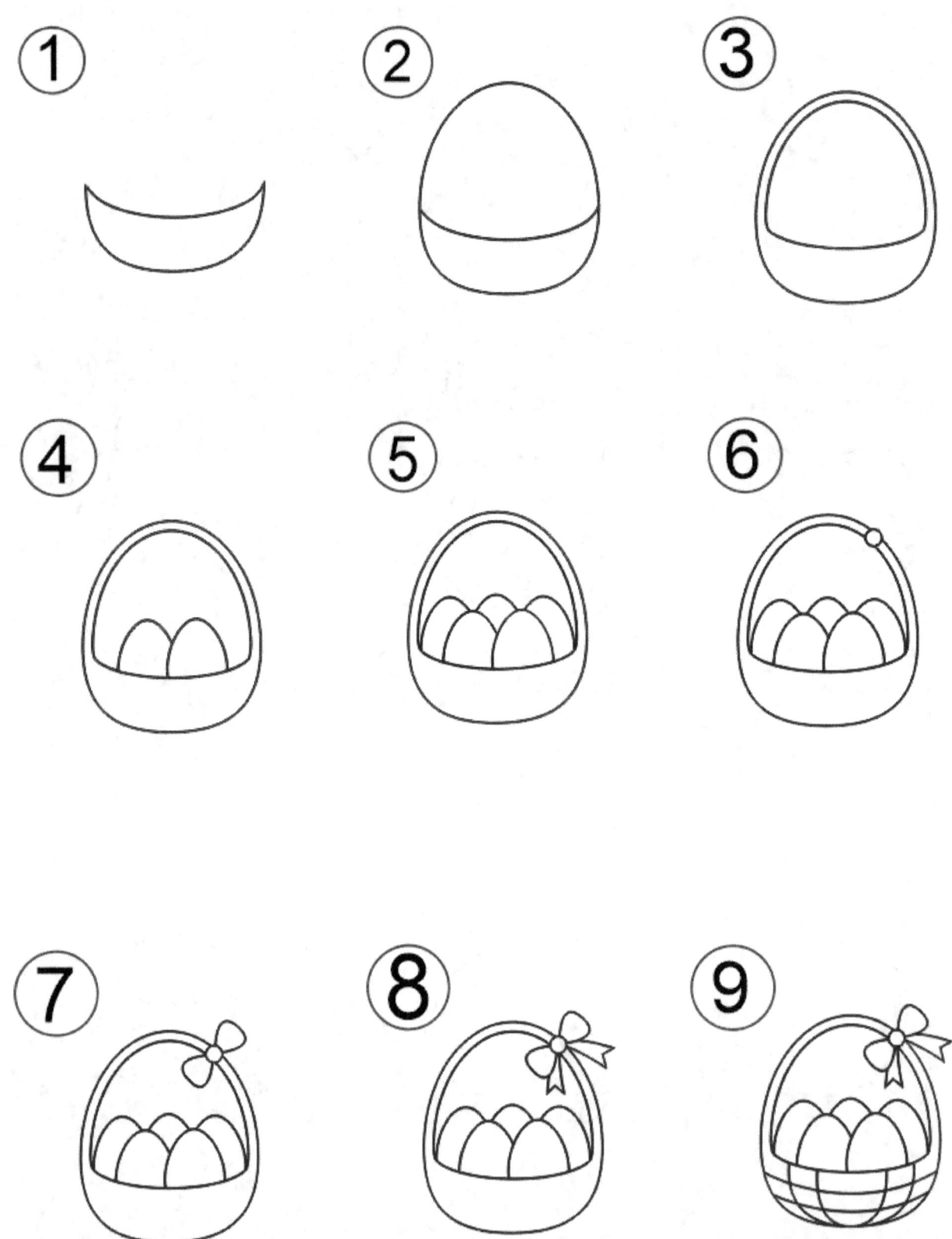

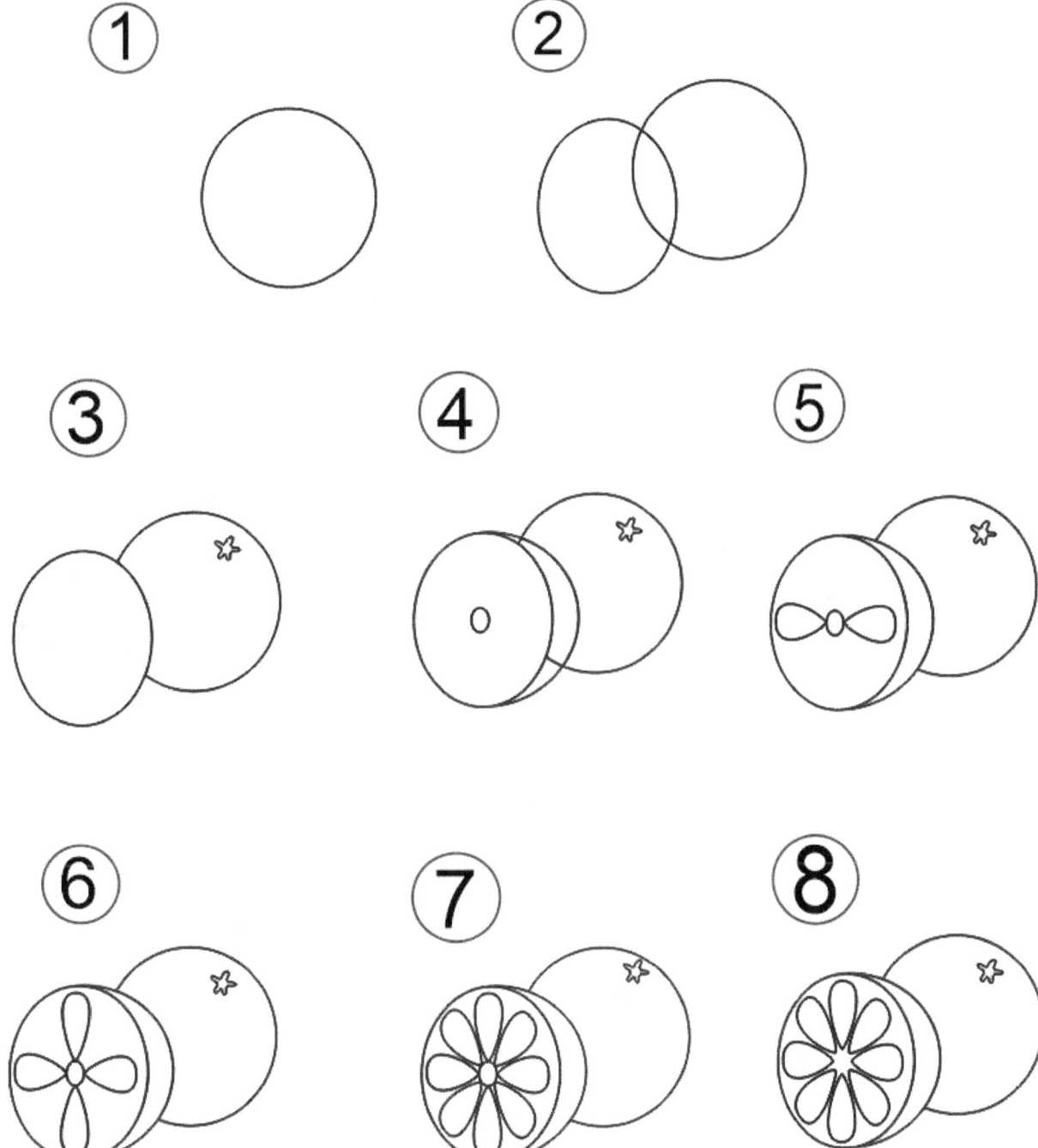

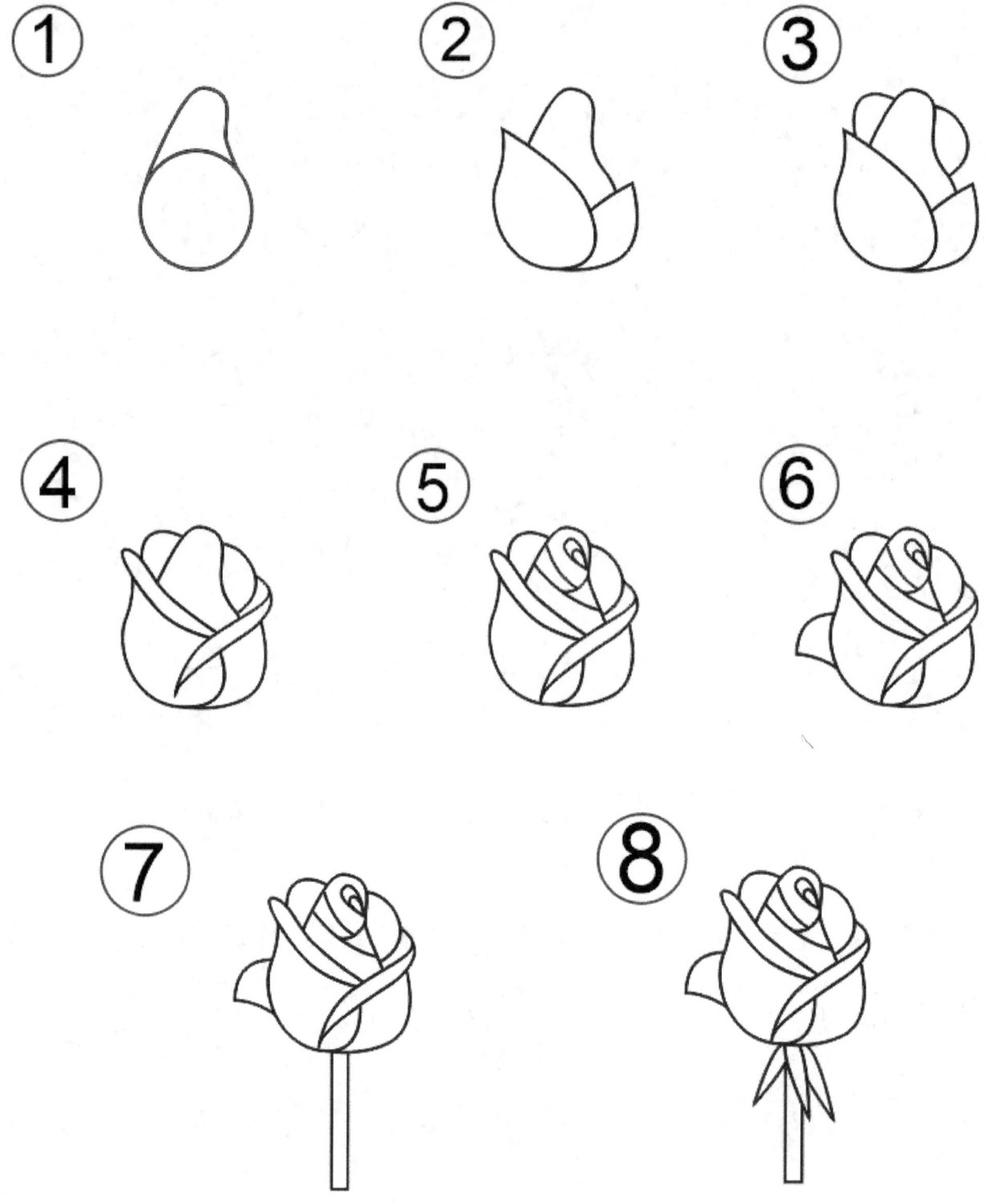

HEN

①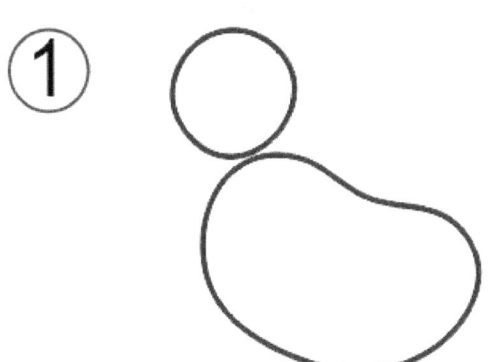

②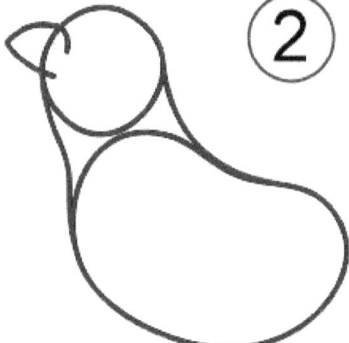

③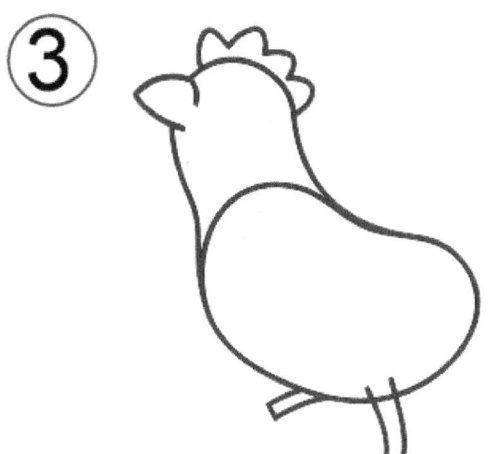

④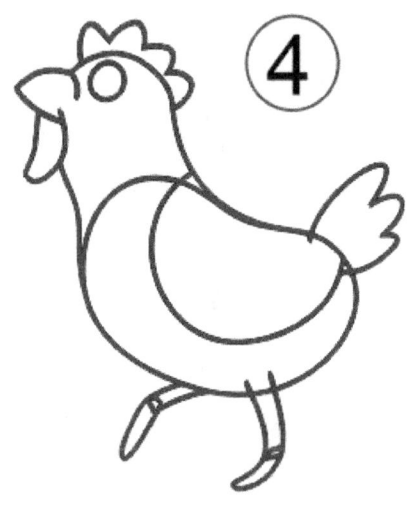

⑤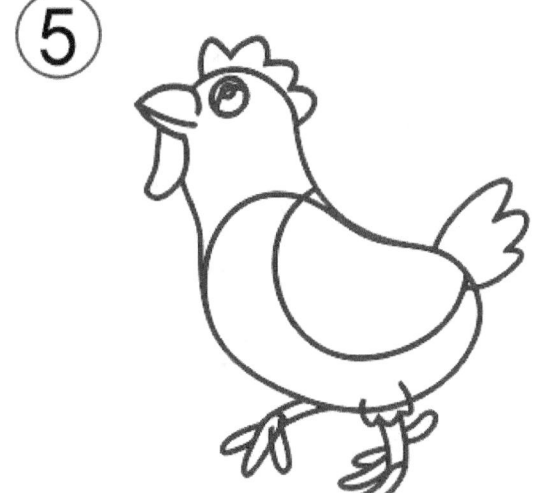

⑥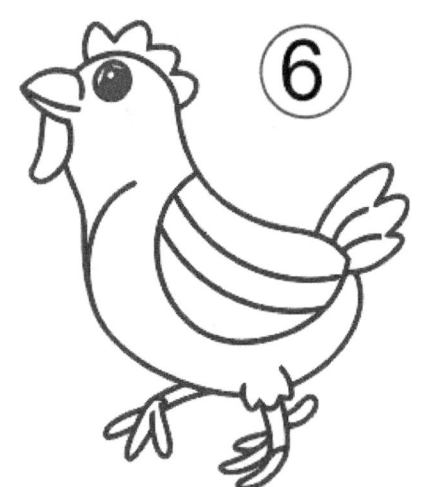

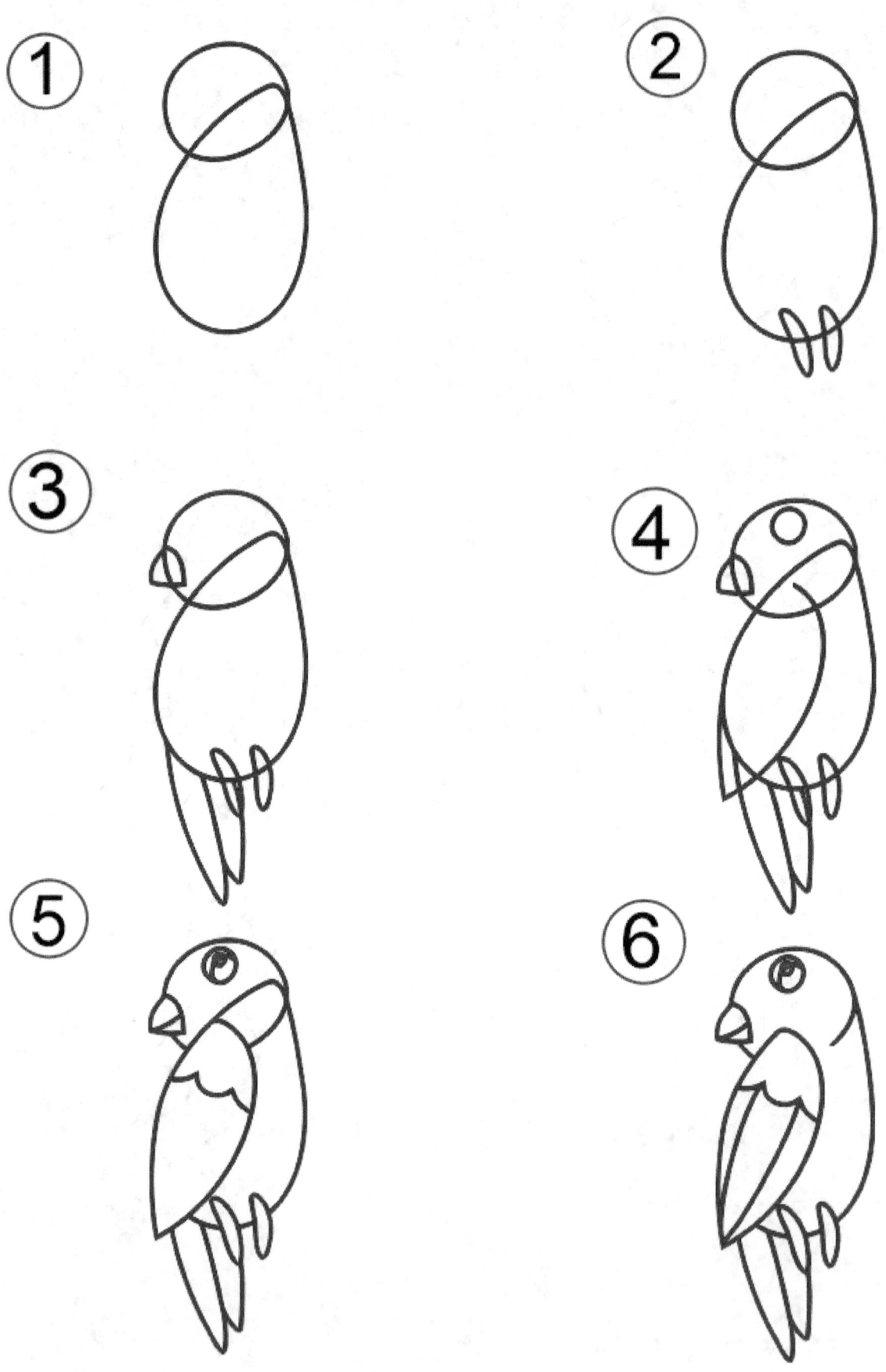

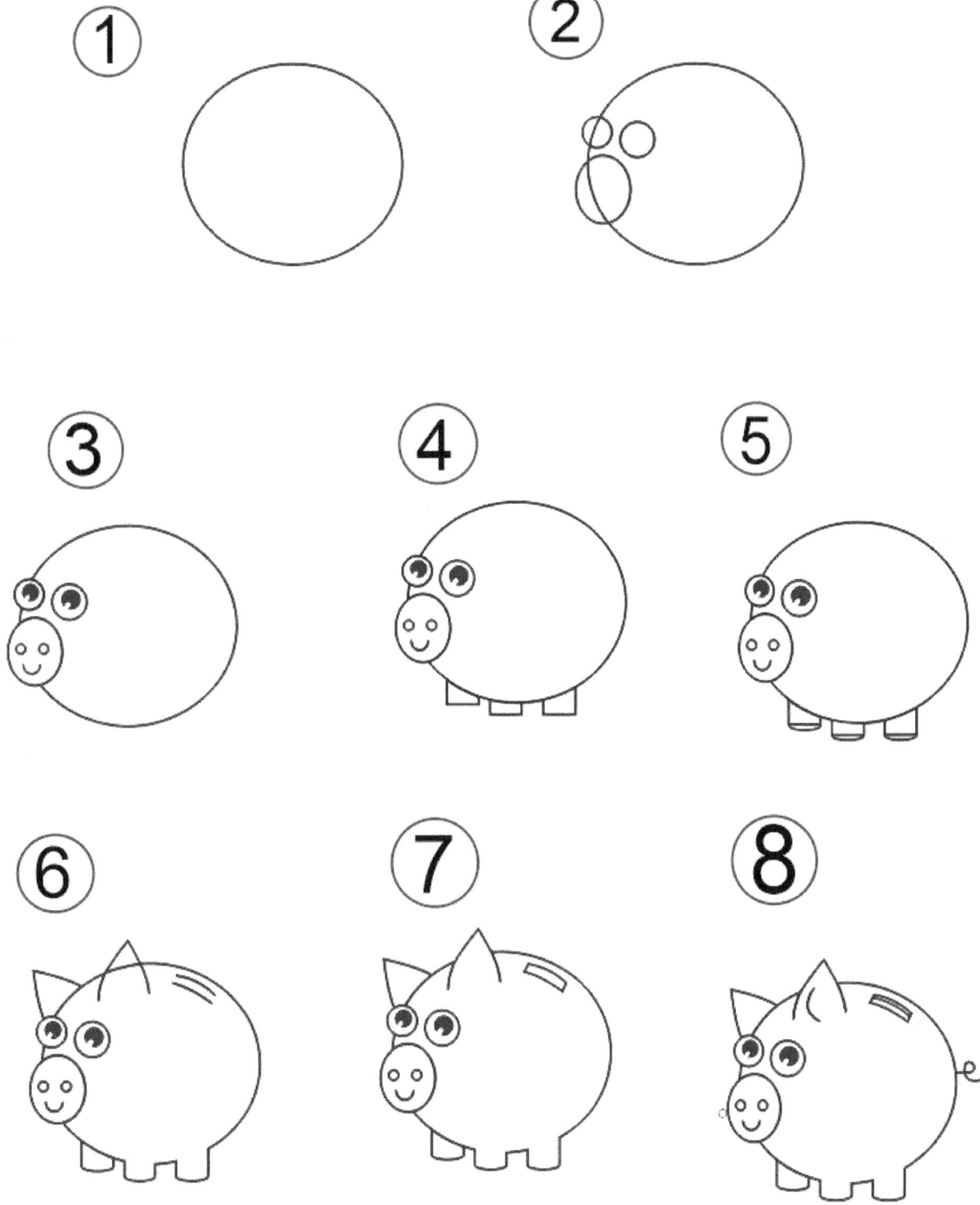

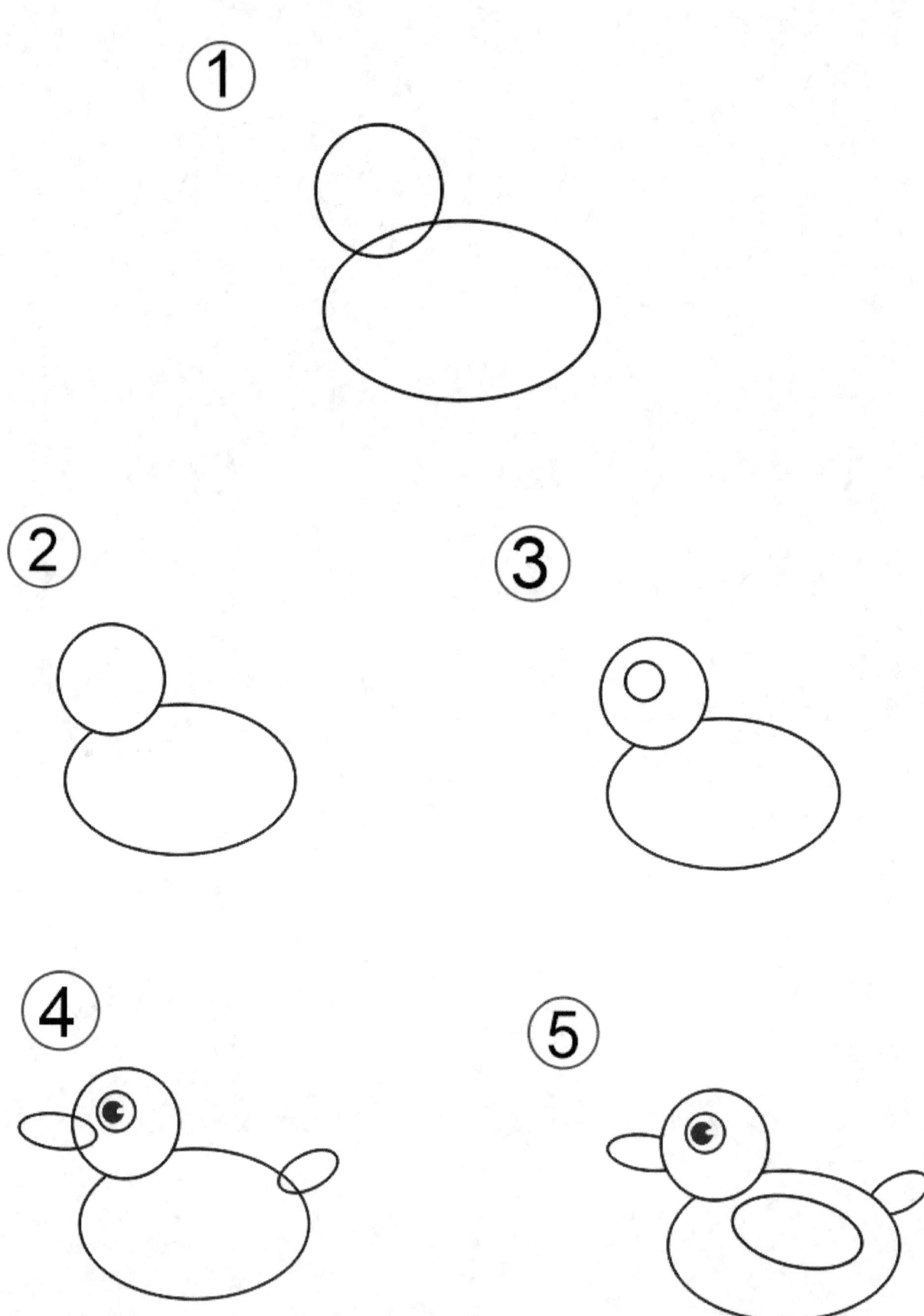

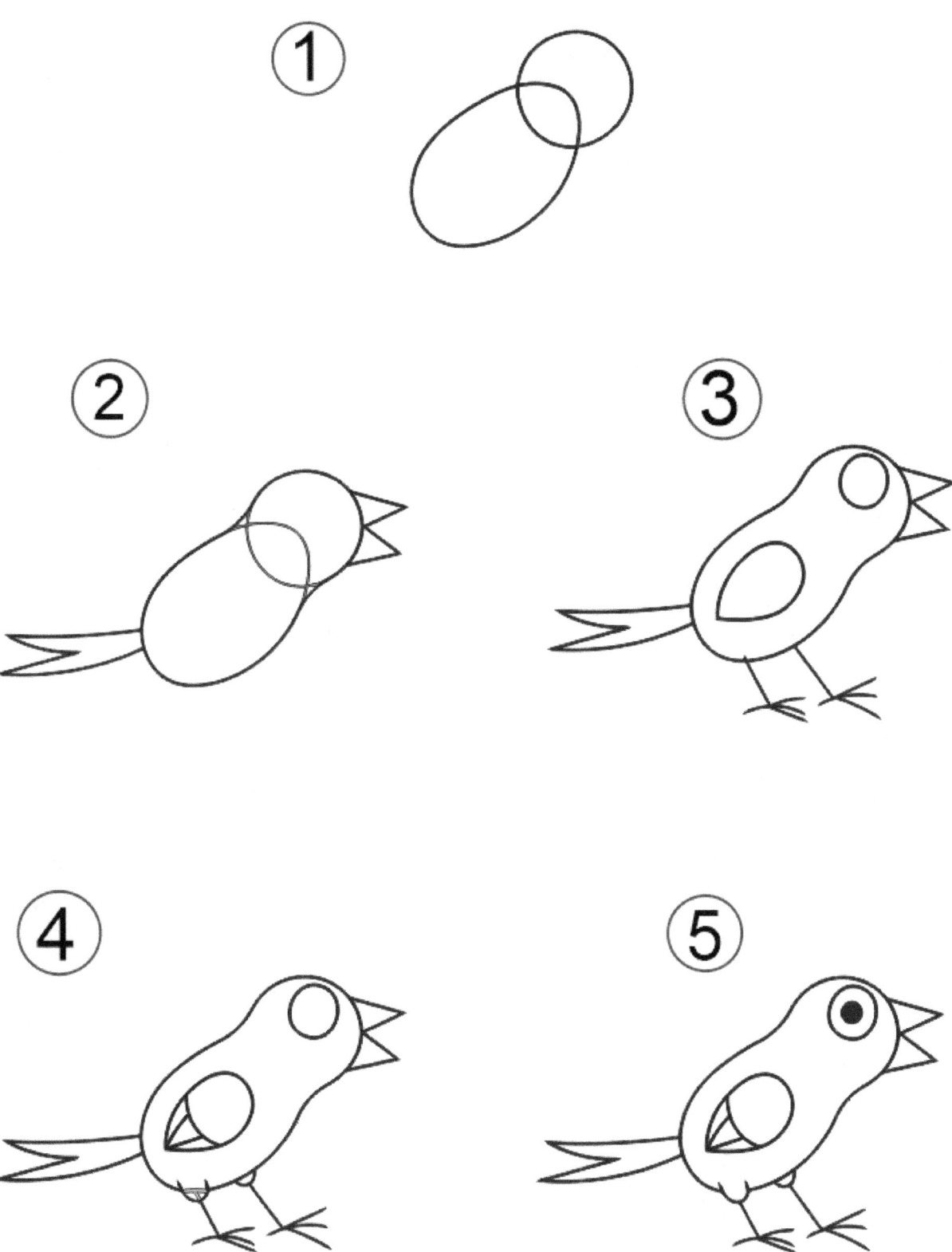

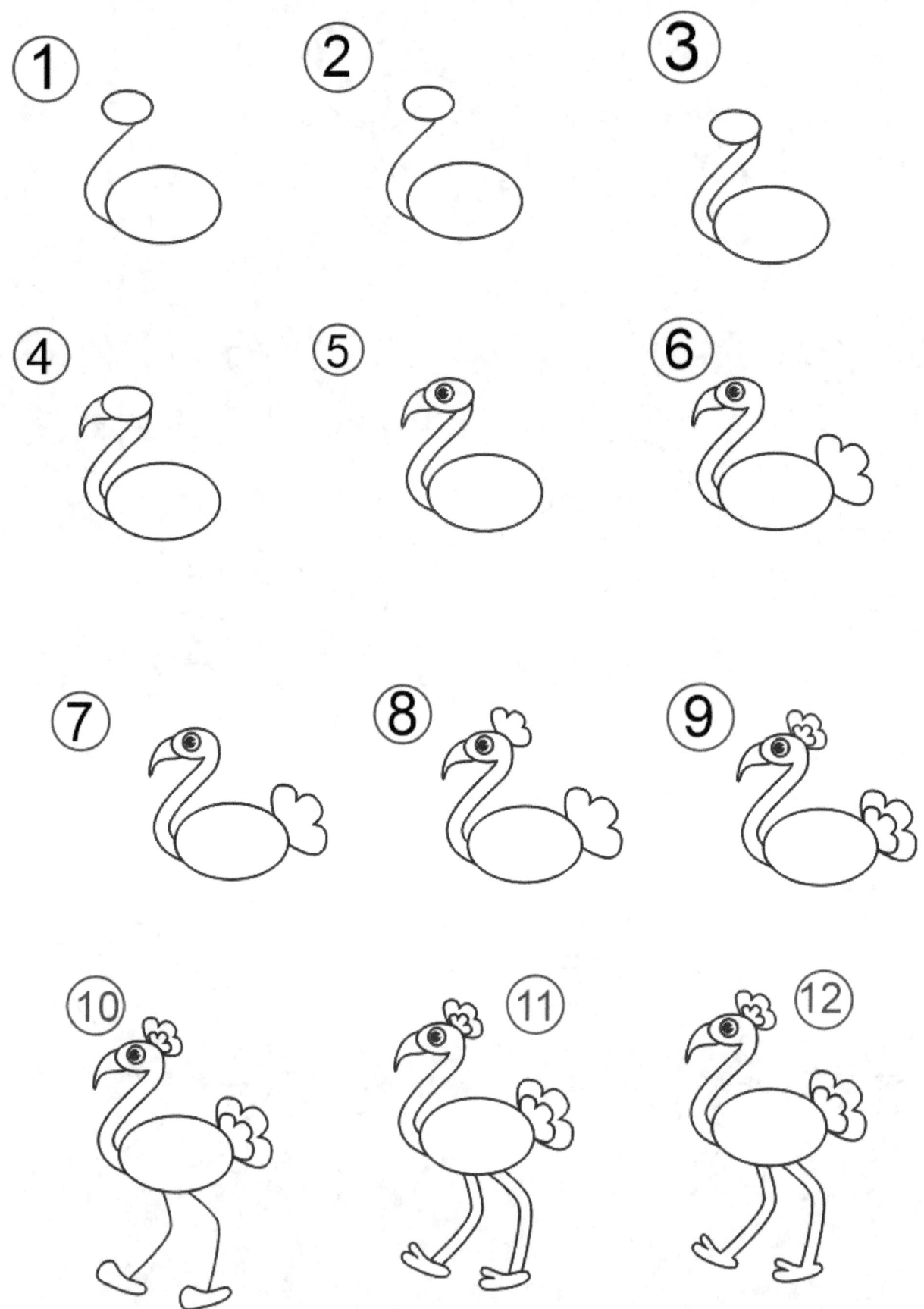

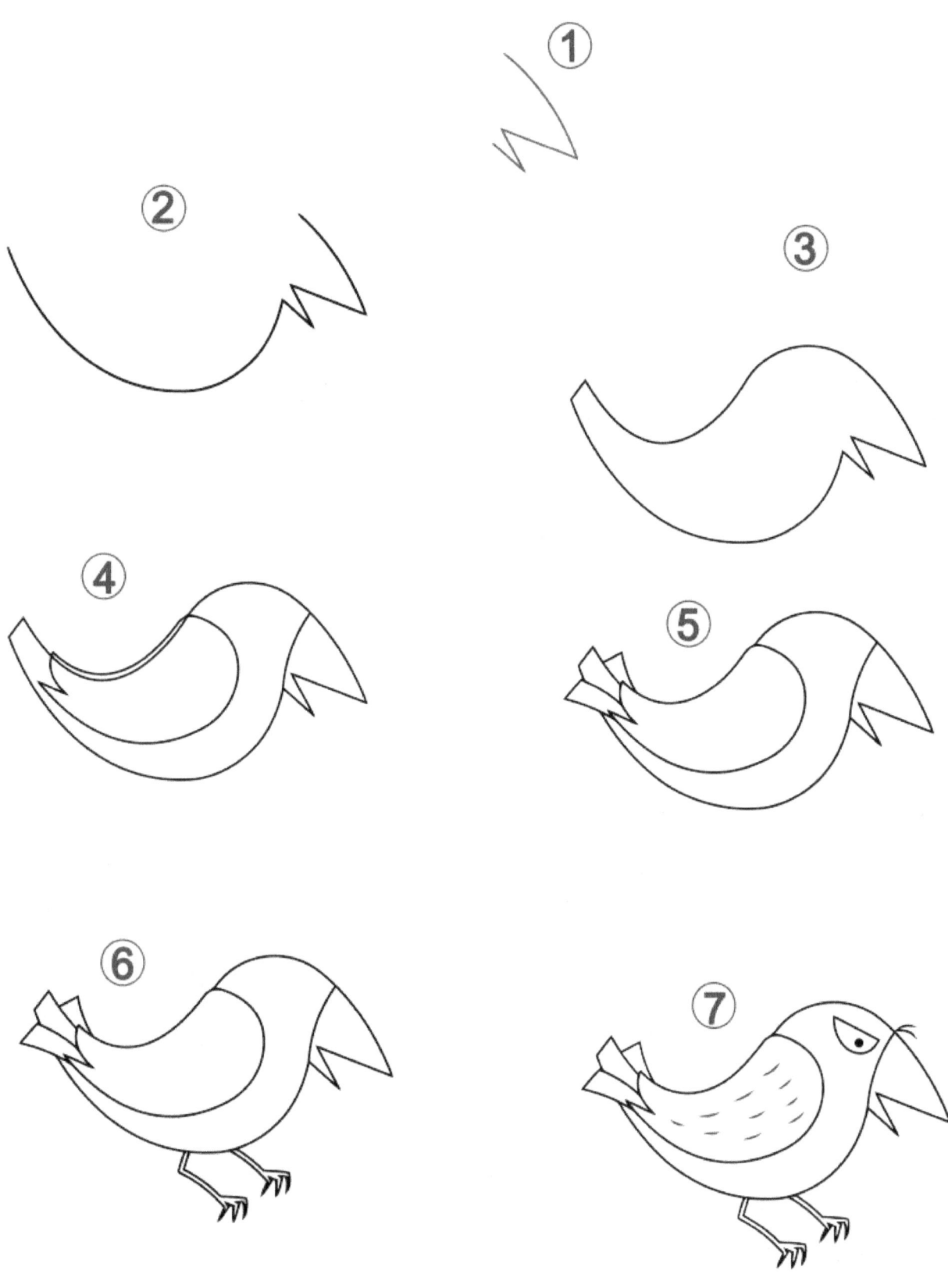

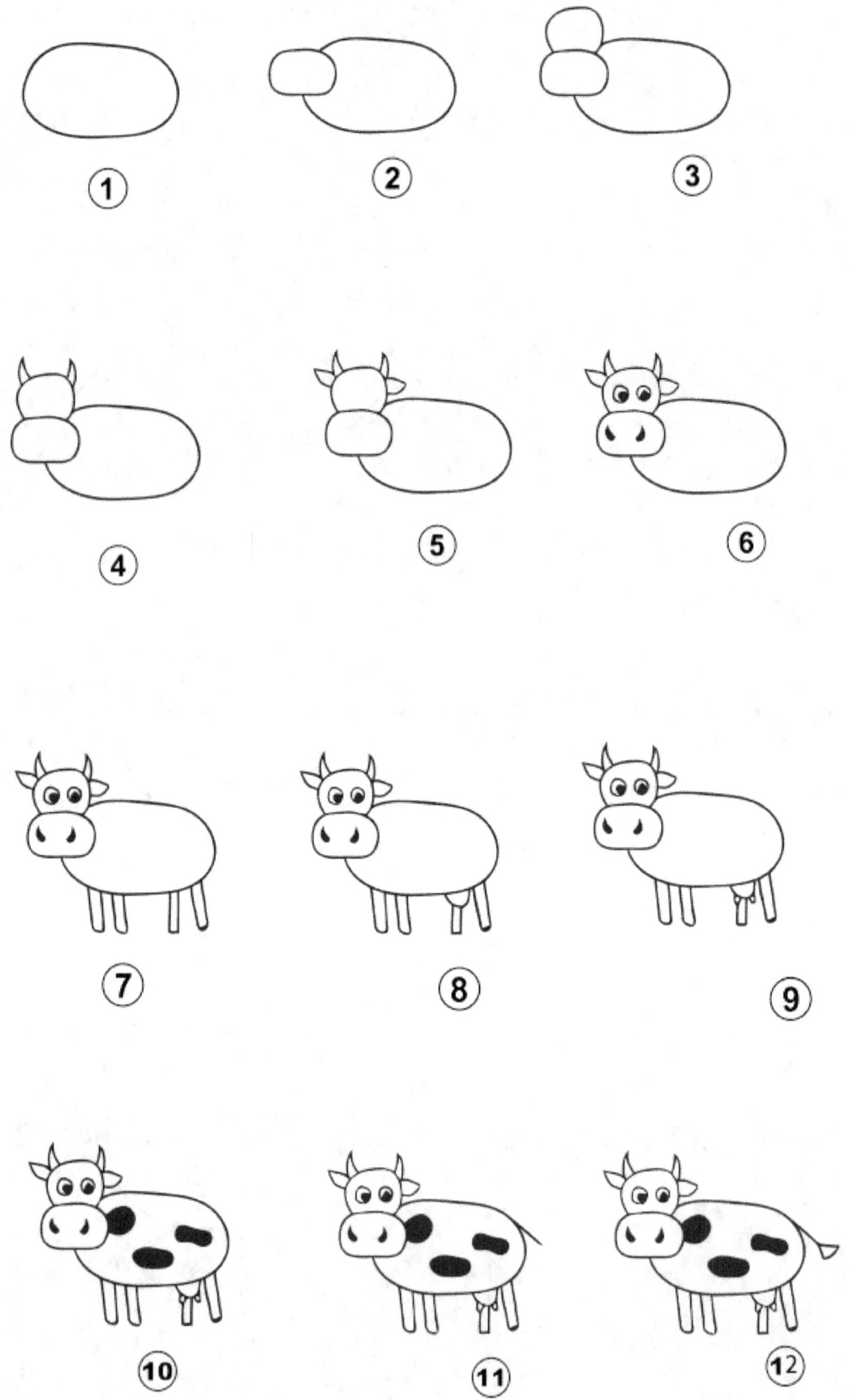

①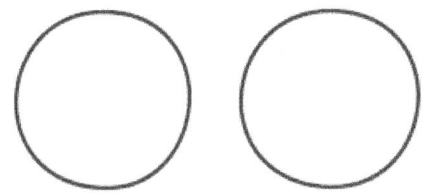

②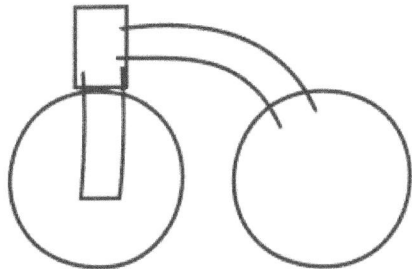

③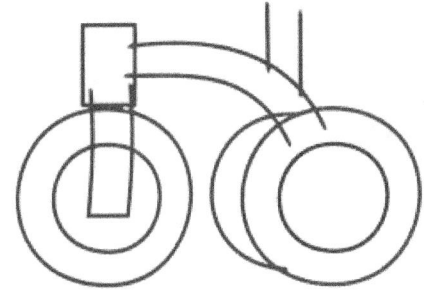

④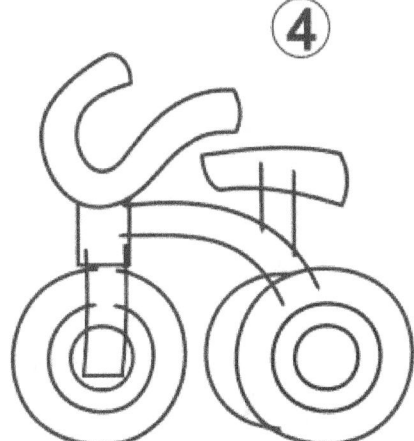

⑤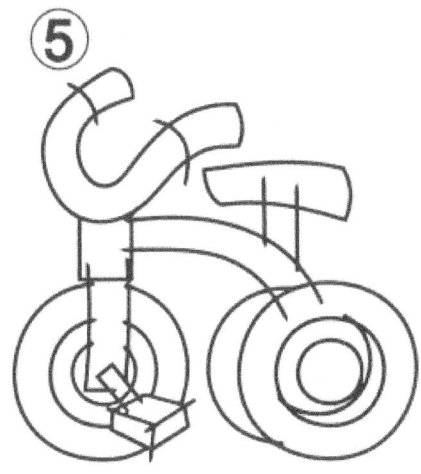

⑥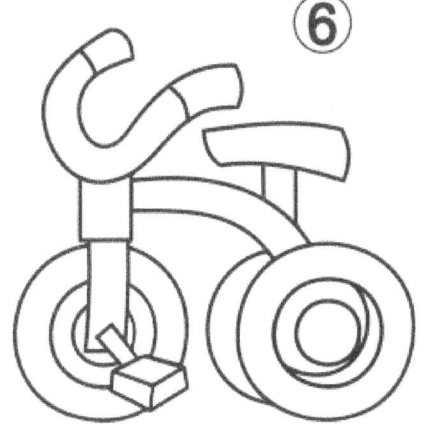

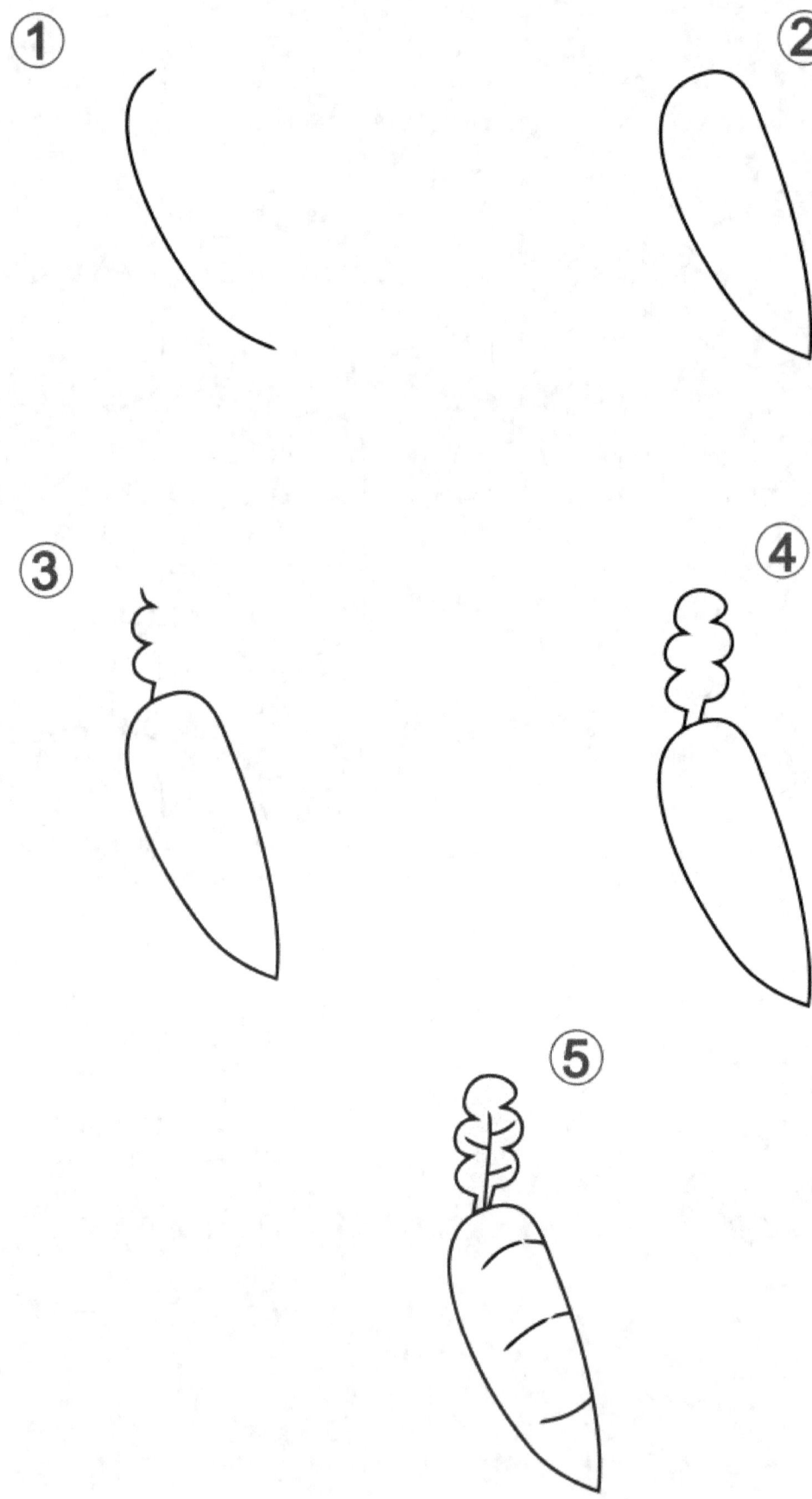

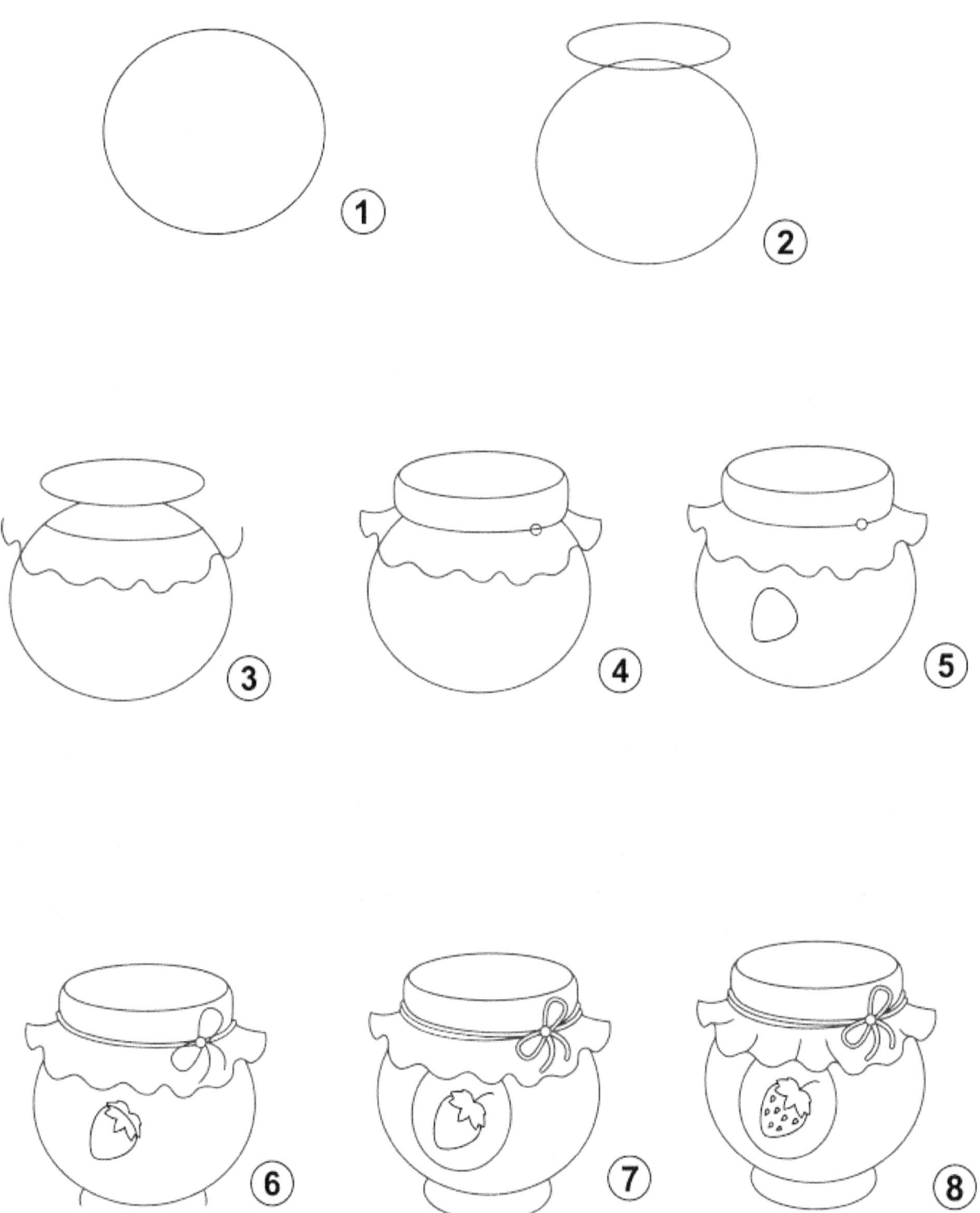

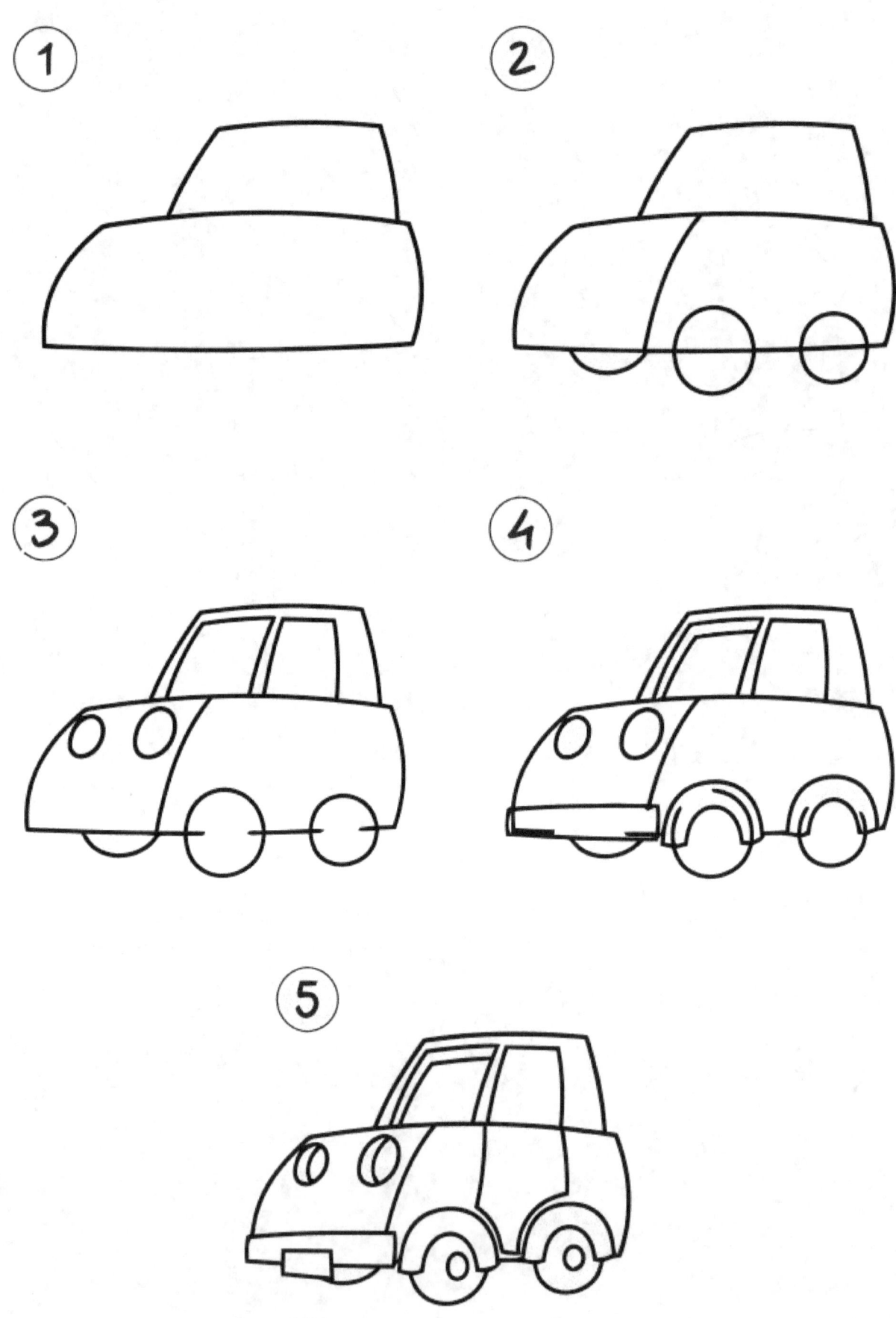

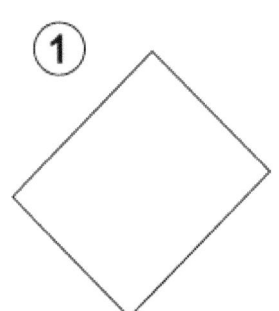

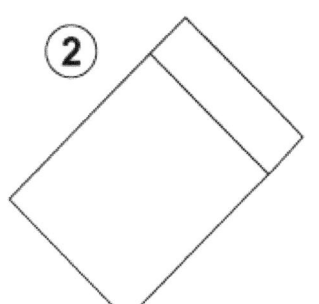

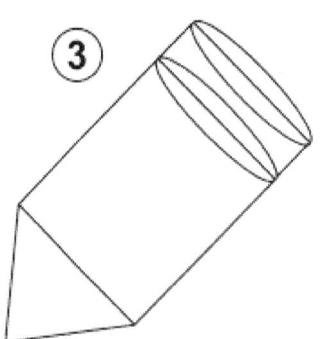

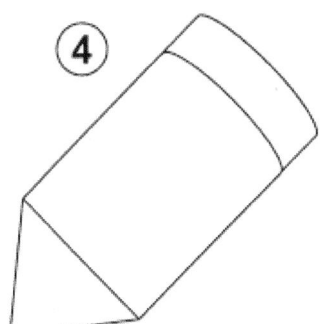

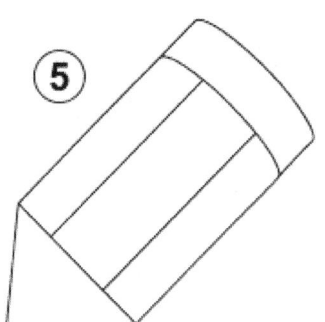

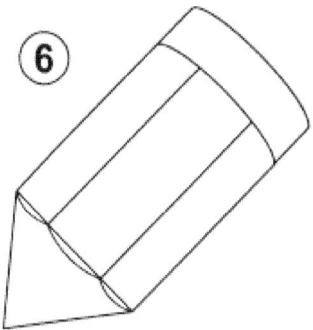

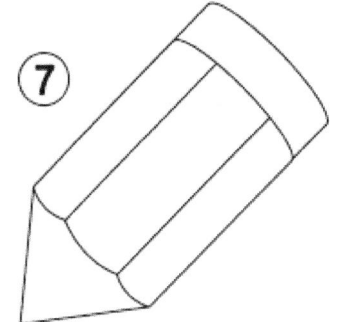

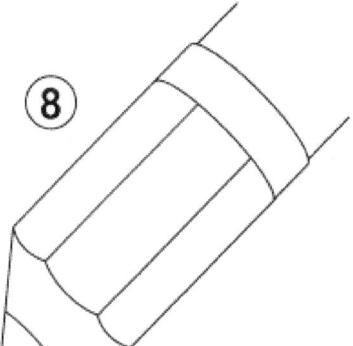

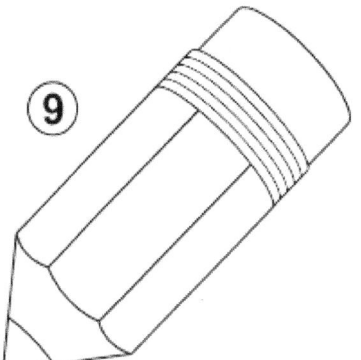

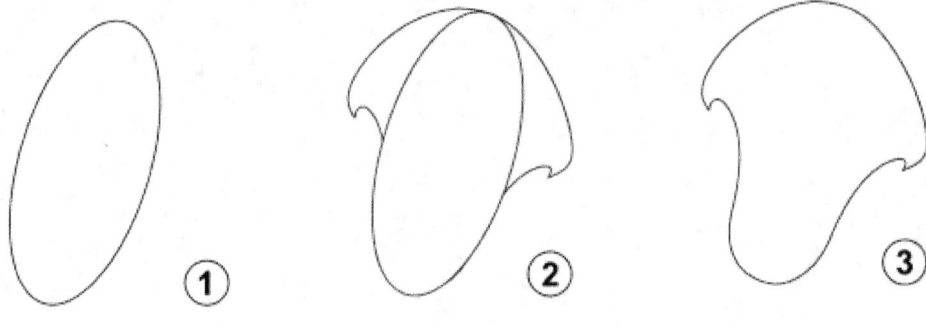

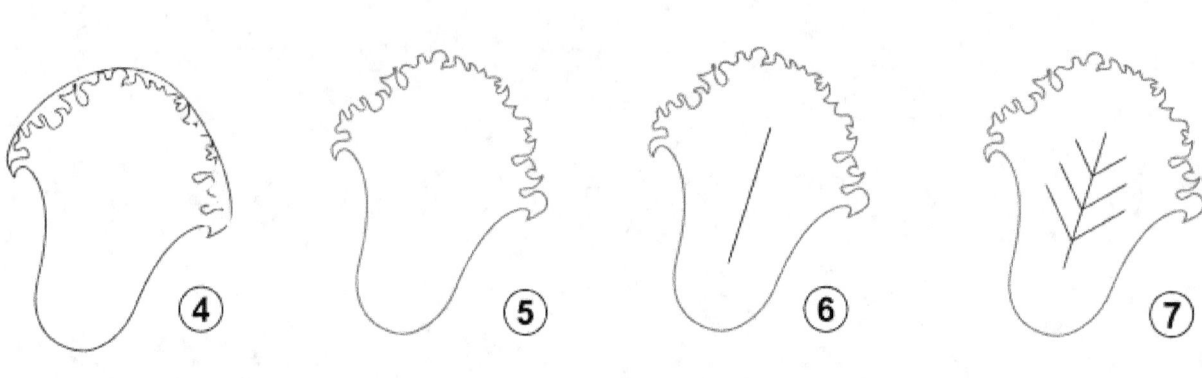

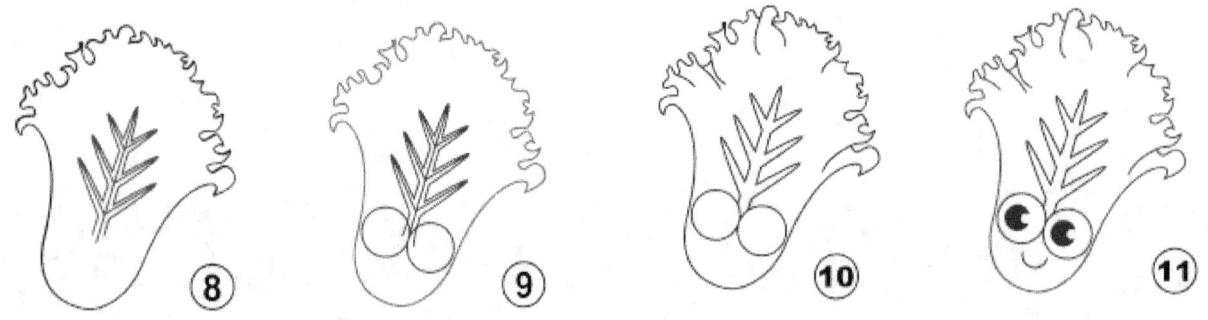

①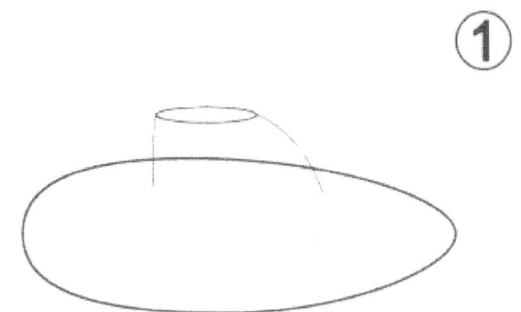

②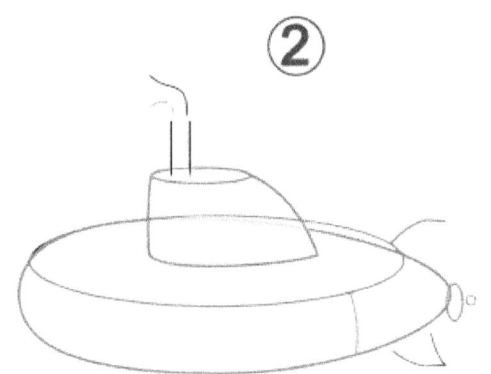

③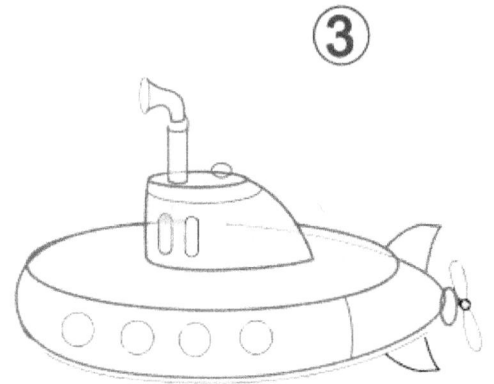

④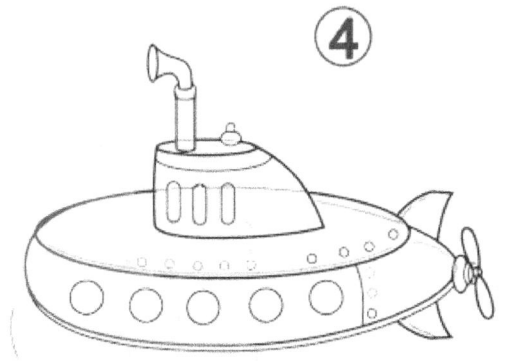

⑤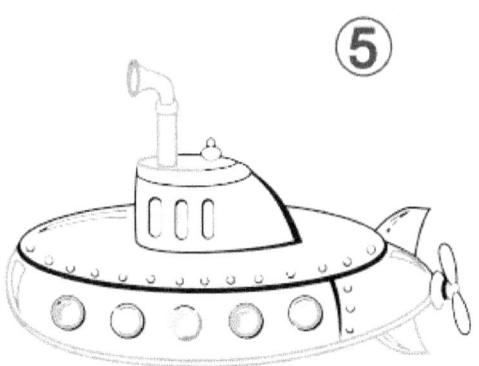

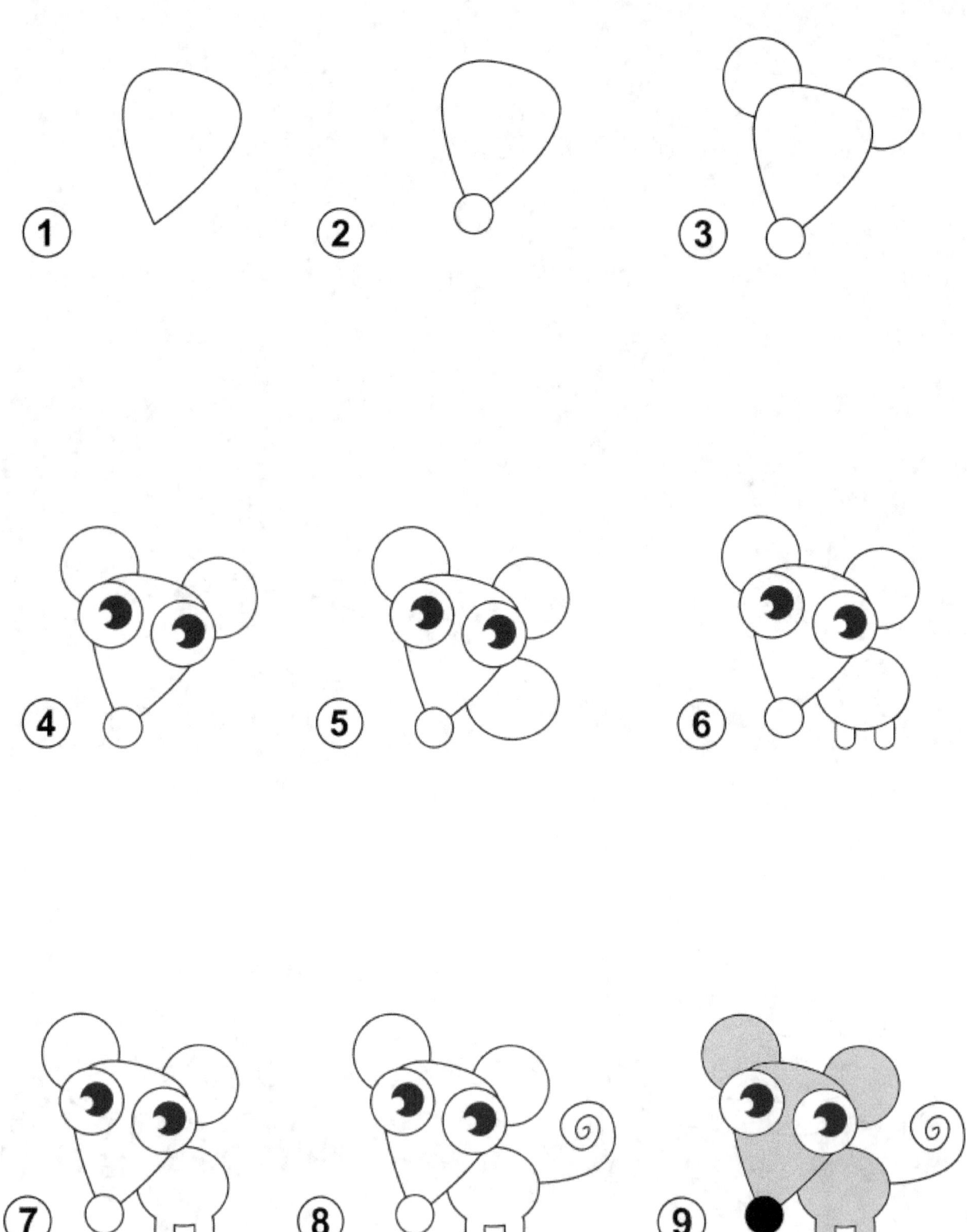

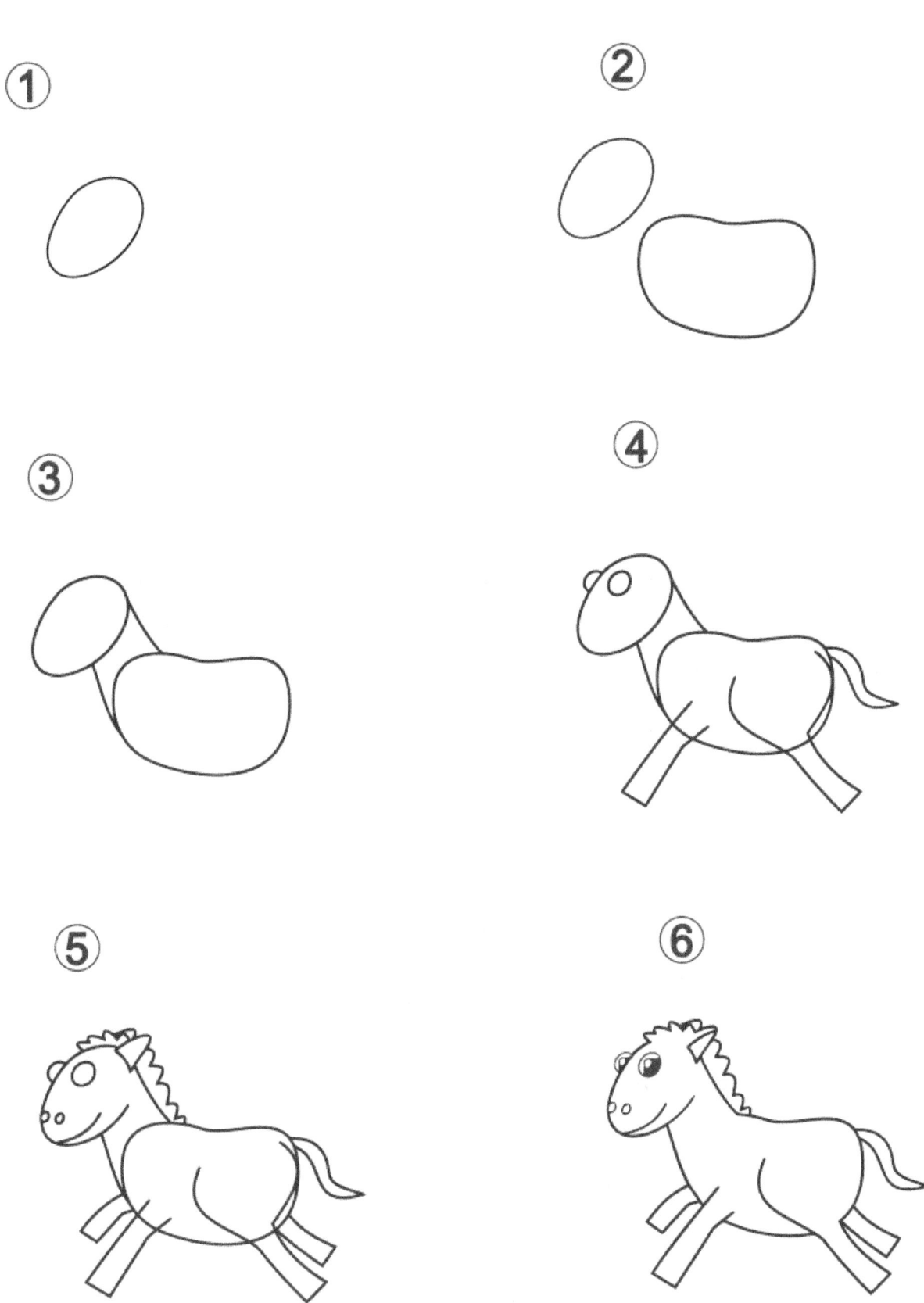

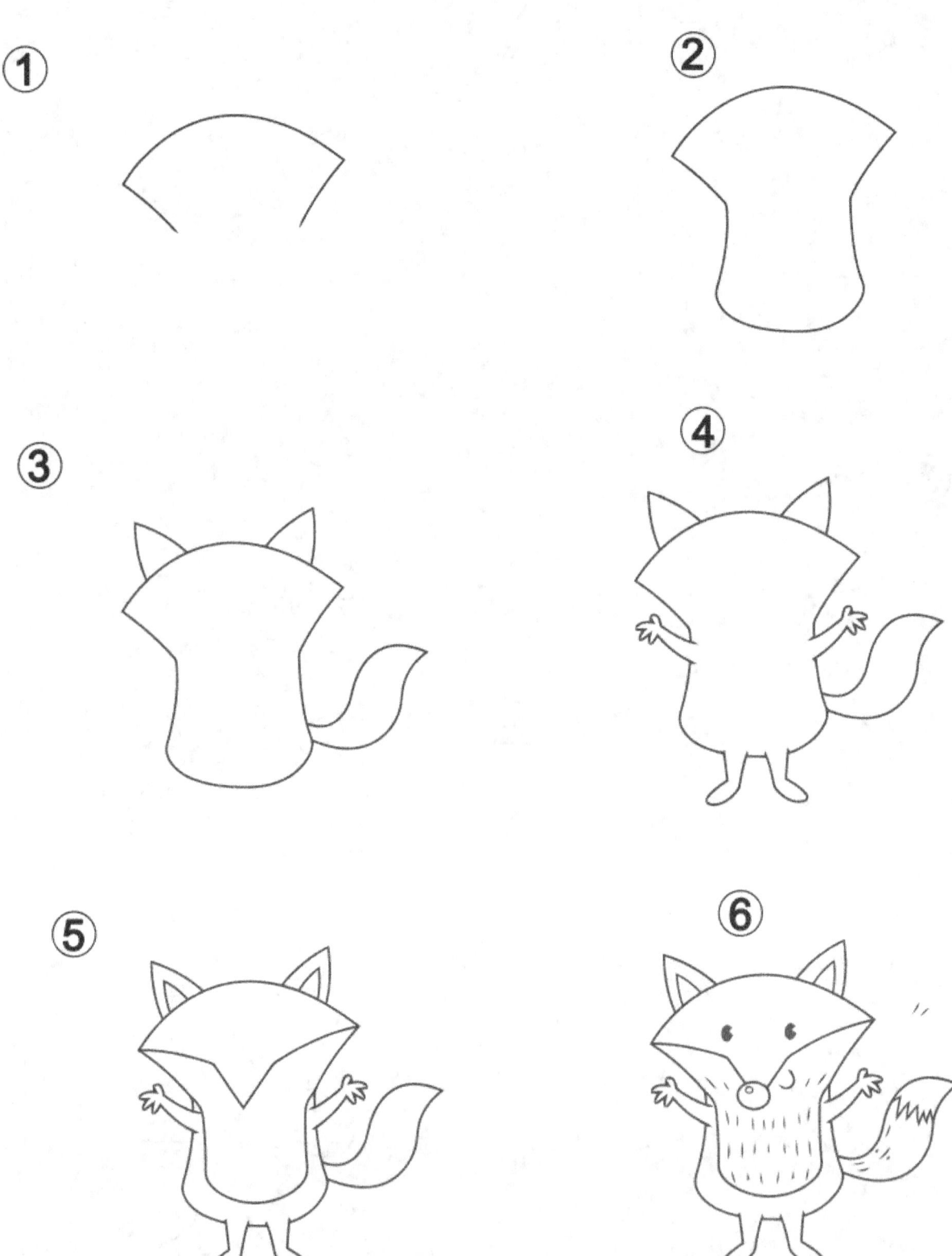

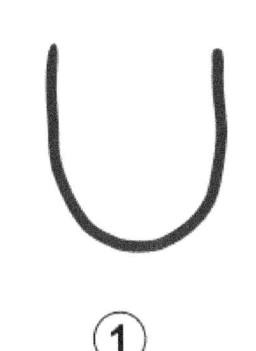

1

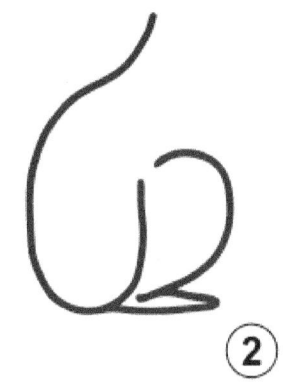

2

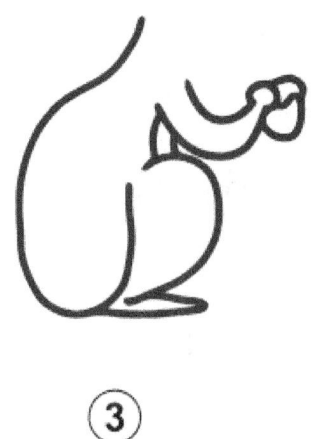

3

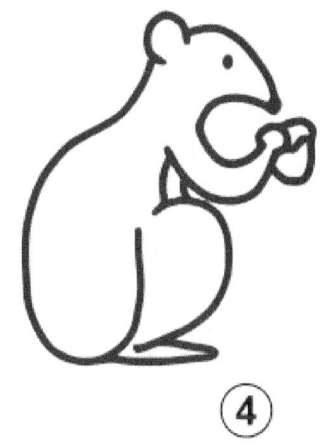

4

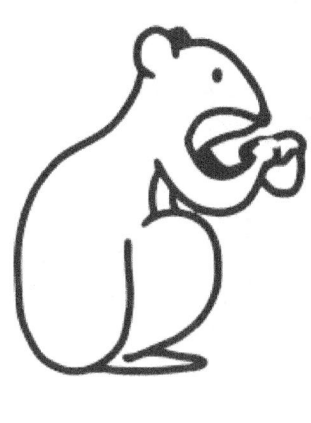

5

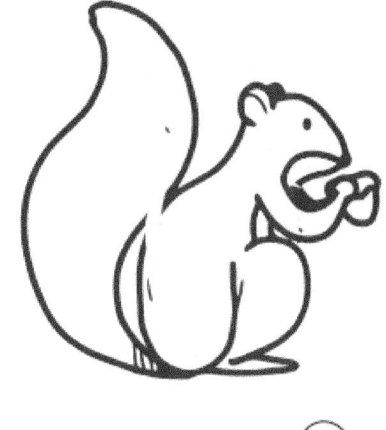

6

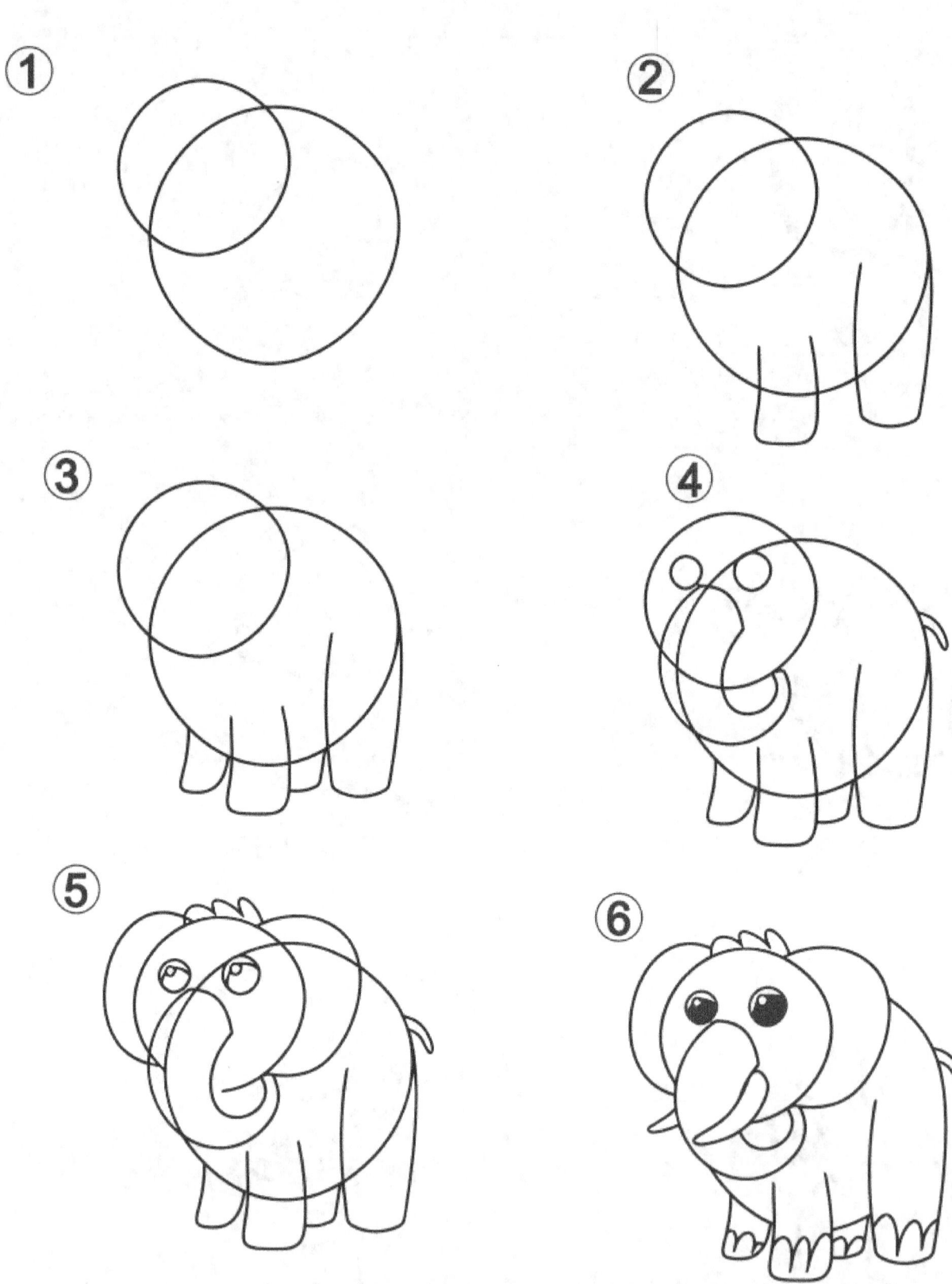

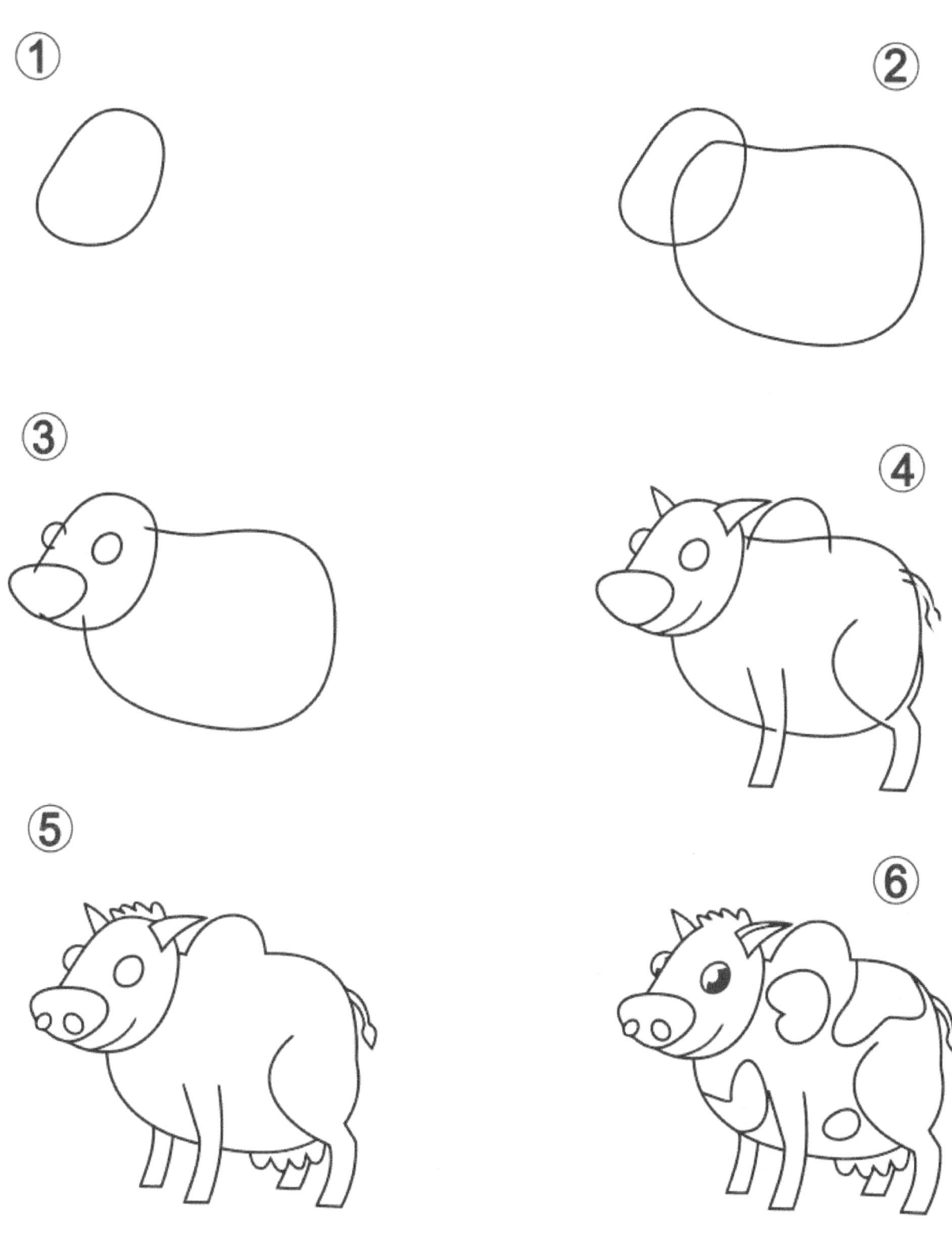

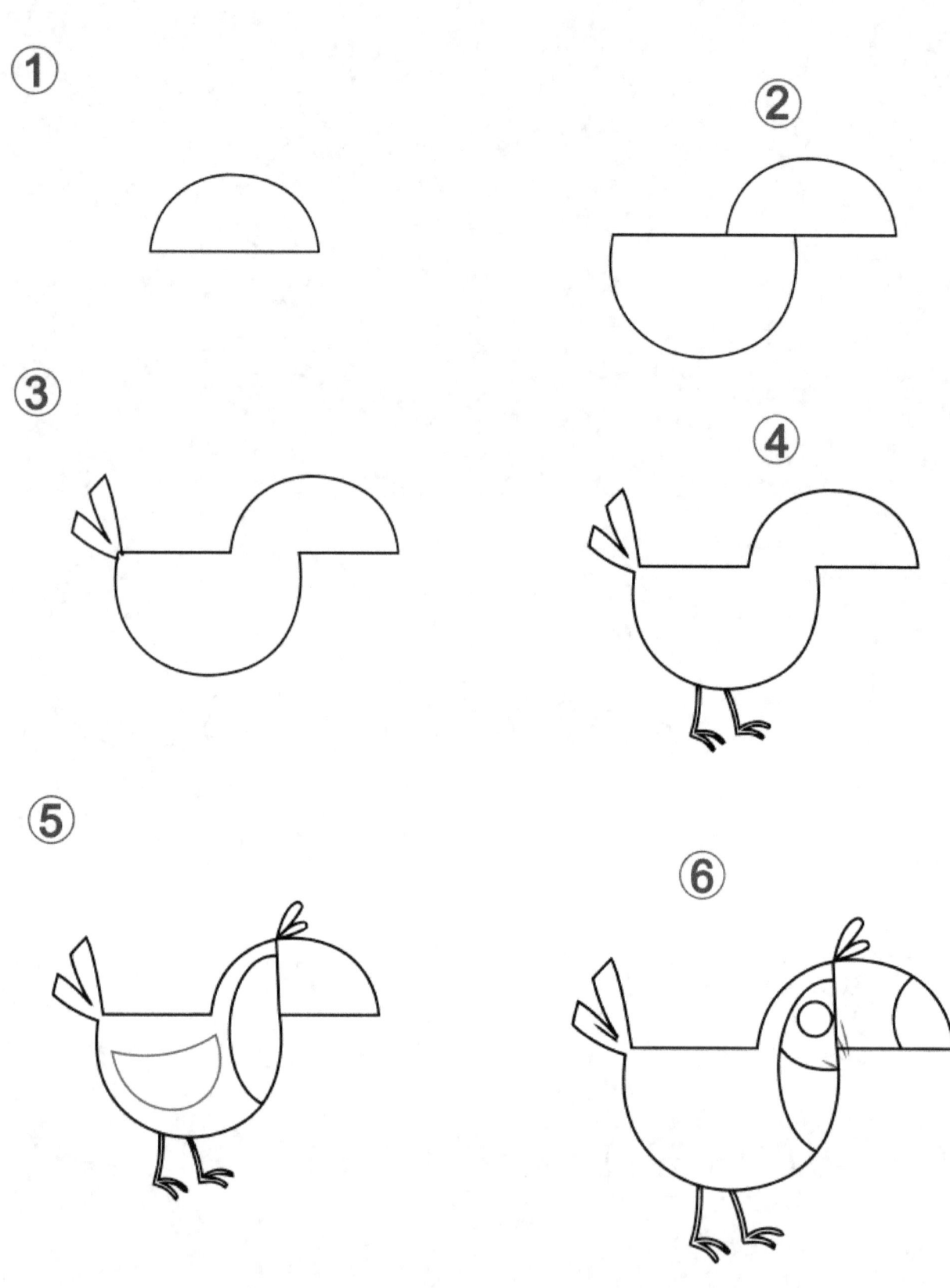

www.ingramcontent.com/pod-product-compliance
Lightning Source LLC
Chambersburg PA
CBHW082218290526
45794CB00009B/3583